THE USE
SYMBOLS IN WORSHIP

The new Alcuin Liturgy Guides revive the tradition of the Alcuin Manual and address both practical and theoretical questions concerning the practice of worship, its setting and celebration. The Liturgy Guides are occasional publications alternating with major liturgical studies in a series known as the Alcuin Collection.

The first two Alcuin Liturgy Guides, *Memorial Services* by Donald Gray, and *Art and Worship* by Anne Dawtry and Christopher Irvine, were published by SPCK in 2002. The third, *Celebrating the Eucharist* by Benjamin Gordon-Taylor and Simon Jones, was published in 2005. Two Liturgy Guides forthcoming in 2008, by Simon Jones and Benjamin Gordon-Taylor, will cover the celebration of the Christian year. The series editor is the Revd Canon Christopher Irvine.

Members of the Alcuin Club receive free copies of the Collection, the Liturgy Guides, and the Joint Liturgical Studies. Founded in 1897, the Alcuin Club seeks to promote the study of Christian liturgy in general, with special reference to worship in the Anglican Communion in particular. The chairman of the Alcuin Club is the Revd Canon Dr Donald Gray CBE, and details regarding membership, the annual subscription and lists of publications can be obtained from the Secretary, Mr Jack Ryding, 'Ty Nant', 6 Parc Bach Trefnant, Denbighshire LL16 4YE.

Visit the Alcuin Club website at **www.alcuinclub.org.uk**

THE USE OF
SYMBOLS IN WORSHIP

Edited by

CHRISTOPHER IRVINE

Alcuin Liturgy Guides 4

First published in Great Britain in 2007

Society for Promoting Christian Knowledge
36 Causton Street
London SW1P 4ST

British Library Cataloguing-in-Publication Data
A catalogue record for this book is available from the British Library.

ISBN 978–0–281–05852–5

1 3 5 7 9 10 8 6 4 2

Typeset by Graphicraft Ltd, Hong Kong
Printed in Great Britain by Ashford Colour Press

Produced on paper from sustainable forests

Contents

Contributors

Sarah Farrimond has been involved in theological education in the Diocese of Wakefield and is an occasional teaching assistant in the Department of Theology and Religious Studies in the University of Leeds. Her research interests include ritual, narrative and the liturgy of marriage. She is currently completing a Ph.D. thesis on these topics for the University of Durham.

Benjamin Gordon-Taylor teaches Liturgical Studies and Ecclesiology at the College of the Resurrection, Mirfield. He is a contributor to *Companion to Common Worship*, vols 1 and 2 (Alcuin Club Collections; SPCK, 2001, 2006), and co-author (with Simon Jones) of *Celebrating the Eucharist* (Alcuin Liturgy Guides 3; SPCK, 2005). His research interests include the theology and language of mystery in relation to liturgy and the liturgical scholarship of Walter Howard Frere. He is a member of the Alcuin Club Committee, and Conference Secretary of the Society for Liturgical Study.

Christopher Irvine was formerly Principal of the College of the Resurrection, Mirfield, and is now a residentiary canon at Canterbury Cathedral. He is a consultant to the Church of England's Liturgical Commission. He co-authored (with Anne Dawtry) *Art and Worship* (Alcuin Liturgy Guides 2; SPCK, 2002), and his most recent book, *The Art of God: The Making of Christians and the Meaning of Worship* (SPCK, 2005), explores the theology of liturgical formation.

Simon Jones is Chaplain and Fellow of Merton College, Oxford, and was formerly a curate in Tewkesbury. He co-authored *Celebrating the Eucharist*, has published work on Dom Gregory Dix, and has also contributed to *Companion to Common Worship*, vols 1 and 2. He is a consultant to the Church of England's Liturgical Commission, and a member of the Alcuin Club Committee.

Preface

[Symbols] both reveal and conceal ... disclosing a different
order of reality and experience. Symbols are thus by definition
mysterious.

Ioan Lewis

This Liturgy Guide arose from an Alcuin Club seminar on liturgical symbols held at the College of the Resurrection, Mirfield
in January 2006. Following the authorization of the whole raft
of *Common Worship* services, some of us felt that we probably
needed to balance this preoccupation with *texts* with that other
vital liturgical language, the use of symbols in worship and in our
pastoral rites. Members of the seminar included our chairman,
the Revd Canon Dr Donald Gray, Fr Benedict Green CR, the
Revd Charles Reid, who presented a key paper on Evangelical views
on the place of symbols in worship, Josephine Evetts Secker, a
Jungian psychotherapist, and the contributors to this volume.
Other conversation partners have also to be thanked for their
encouragement and comments on earlier drafts, especially Dr
Juliette Day, Dr John Melloh of the University of Notre Dame,
and Fr George Guiver CR.

In the first chapter I attempt to set the place of symbols
in the context of our contemporary culture and to elucidate an
understanding of liturgical symbols. More generally, our aim
in Chapters 2 to 6 has been to provide in each chapter some
theological and historical background to the relevant symbols
and then to offer some very practical guidance as to the place
and use of symbols in the whole range of *Common Worship* services. Twenty-five years ago it was common to speak of a 'crisis
of symbolism'. Today the cultural ground has shifted, and in
our postmodern, technological age there seems to be a new
fascination with symbols. This shift has prompted us to press
for a greater understanding of the place of symbols in a visual

age of instant global communication and global brands. Indeed, the media are so saturated with mesmerizing visual images that arguably the relationship between image and reality is becoming increasingly distorted, particularly as we find ourselves occupying a number of 'virtual worlds'. In all this there is a real danger of losing the sense of our connectedness with others and with the mystery of God in Christ. Liturgical symbols are not simply visual aids or unequivocal signs referring to single, simple realities, but are suggestive and evocative. Such symbols belong to a whole matrix of imagery in scripture and in the prayer texts which accompany the ritual acts of worship.

Never before in the history of the Church of England's authorized services have we seen such scope for the use of symbols in worship and in our pastoral rites as that which is found in the family of *Common Worship* services. But as Simon Jones notes in Chapter 3, the directions in the service texts and the official commentaries are not as clear or as consistent as they might be. Furthermore, we are also aware of the increasing interest in the use of symbols in worship, and of how this interest is to be found across the whole spectrum of ecclesial traditions and denominations, and this again places another demand upon those who lead worship, namely a particular competence and confidence in handling symbols. Of course those who lead worship must first know what it is to be a worshipper, and have some sense of the power of symbols within a liturgical context. Our growth in such a desired liturgical sensibility is a key element not only in our own liturgical formation, but in the very formation of the people of God, and therefore ought to be high on the agenda of the Church today. This challenge was presented by the critic Nicholas Lezard in a recent book review (*Guardian*, 7 January 2006) in which he commented on a banal sermon illustration he had recently heard and lamented how in our own day we are deprived of a deep level of symbolic significance in the very areas of life where it is most needed and would be most appreciated. This challenge needs to be heeded urgently if our worship is to communicate the deep things of the Spirit.

Furthermore, at a time when the Church is rightly preoccupied with mission, we must also reckon with the ways in which a well-prepared and sensitively celebrated liturgical rite (whether it is a celebration of the Word, a baptism, or a funeral) affects those who have gathered for the occasion. Very often, especially in our pastoral rites, liturgical actions can speak powerfully in ways which cannot always be easily articulated or expressed. Indeed, the fact that people might not always be able to put into words the ways in which services have affected them might remind us that our liturgical symbols may well speak to people in a *pre-conscious* way. Explanations and attempts to deepen faith certainly need to occur, but preferably not during worship, and we should look for other contexts and opportunities to do this, such as parish discussion groups and Lent courses. We cannot expect liturgy to deliver everything all at once. As I argued in *The Art of God* (Irvine 2005), our formation as Christians takes time, and yet those very occasions when we gather with others consciously before the mystery of God are privileged occasions when God seeks to shape us more closely, through the Spirit, into the likeness of Christ. In the end, perhaps it is a Church shaped by its worship that will be the most effective mission-shaped Church in and for the world.

The contributors to this Guide are teachers of worship and liturgical theology, and like all those who teach we recognize how much we gain from those whom we teach, and it is to them that we dedicate this book. I would particularly like to thank Alex Faludy for his account of the Hungarian 'Candlelight Revolution' which is referred to in Chapter 4, and Tracy Charnock for her appreciation of the symbolic dimension of the practice of liturgy.

Christopher Irvine

1

The language of symbols

CHRISTOPHER IRVINE

Our cultural context

In our increasingly visual culture, signs, signals and visual icons assault us at every turn, each competing for our attention, and subtly shaping our understanding of the kind of world we live in and what we might aspire to have and be. They function both as landmarks, helping us to place ourselves in our social world, and as signals, calling for a predetermined pattern of action and behaviour. Indeed, in any society, its signs and symbols project what that society is. But exactly what kind of social world is it that is projected through the complexities of modern technology and manipulated by the media and the market-place?

A feature of contemporary life much commented upon is globalization, a complex phenomenon driven largely by the ever-expanding market economy. And what we see here is the economic colonization of the 'global village' through large western multi-national corporations, from oil companies to fast-food outlets, each pushing their corporate logo and trademarks. The successful marketing of goods requires easy and immediate recognition from consumers, hence the importance of striking visual signs indicating a particular brand or manufacturer. The design and display of brand names and goods belongs to the advertising industry, whose success wholly lies in its ability to catch our attention and persuade us that the commodity or service they display is vital for our comfort, entertainment or well-being. To maintain their hold on the market organizations and manufacturing companies continually have to re-present themselves, re-brand their product, and design new logos to hold the attention of the market. But it is not only goods that are re-branded. Individuals too can reinvent themselves, find a new style, or have a complete makeover. We don't all need to consult an image consultant, or a personal life-style guru, to find a new and striking image to make a visual statement about who we are, or what it is that we are wanting to sell. The images are already there, displayed in every public space from the walls of the Tube platform to hoardings on the street corner. Advertising continuously bombards us with images and icons. Indeed, one might say that the market economy trades as much in visual images and symbols as it does in hard currency and financial exchange.

Globalization is undoubtedly a puzzling phenomenon and one that is troublingly paradoxical. Information technology is another feature of globalization, and we are only beginning to grasp the implications and effects of e-mail and the Internet. Wherever you live, you can access the World Wide Web and immediately download images and information. The other side of the world is literally just a click away. And yet, ethnic, tribal and religious tensions are fatally fracturing the world and dividing communities, and the images of tribal conflicts, famine and natural disaster which constantly flash on to our screens explode the illusion that we are indeed living in 'one world'. The technological achievement of providing instant communication in one sense does bring us all closer, but possibly at the cost of overriding cultural diversity and concealing the deeper divisions and inequalities within the global village.

Communications looms large in our high-tech world. It is not only big business, but increasingly a subject of academic study and critical theory. In the complex field of linguistics, for instance, we can detect a growing sense of the symbolic nature of human communication. Language itself, the most basic means of communication, is seen in terms of semiotics, of the making, sending and decoding of signs. The basic units of communication (individual words, or even their component sounds, 'morphemes') are understood as being signifiers, and the perceived world itself as being constituted by what is signified by language. The exchange of significance in our use of language is notoriously complex, and further, we all know that successful communication requires one's interlocutors not only to 'read' what we say in speech or written word, but also to pick up, as we might say, all the signals.

Social commentators often point to the ubiquity of advertising and media saturation as features of contemporary life, but when we add the complexities of communications to this picture we can see that our social world is symbolically constructed and maintained through an intricate web of signs, signals and icons. Interestingly the terminology here uncovers yet another irony of modernity, of how an increasingly secular society trades on the traditional vocabulary of religious belief and practice. The language of signs, for instance, has its roots in the acts of the Hebrew prophets, who figured God's unfolding purpose in dramatic gesture, object and word; and again, before computer-speak, 'icons' referred simply to images of holy figures, like Mary, or episodes of salvation history, like the Transfiguration. In our contemporary visual culture, our icons are the icons of the screen, the football pitch, the fashion industry, and are perniciously unmasked by the media and publicity exposure as quickly as they are made. These icons are superficial and shifting digital images refracted through the media, and have more to do with ephemeral appearance than personal presence. In striking contrast to this, traditional religious images, such as the famous Rublev icon of the Trinity, are understood to mediate a depth of being. The icons we see in a worship setting are an integral part of the whole apparatus of worship, a vital visual element in the whole complex symbolic system which, we will argue, constitutes an act of worship.

A symbolic world

One might reasonably assume that the use of symbols in worship belongs to those traditions of liturgical practice which are sacramental in emphasis, such as the Catholic tradition in Anglicanism, Roman Catholicism, and the Eastern Orthodox and oriental Churches. But this is a questionable and rather restrictive assumption, for the place of symbols can also be detected in those worship traditions which have disavowed ceremony and focus primarily on the written and spoken word. I can recall an occasion when, as a visiting preacher at a United Reformed church, I commented on the lack of ritual and symbolic focus to the minister and was properly corrected for failing to see the explicit ritual action which had preceded the service. After the vestry prayer an elder had led the minister into the church carrying the Bible, a focused and deliberate ritual act, demonstrating the highly charged symbolic significance of the Bible as the Word of God. Only when the Bible had been placed on the reading desk could the congregation be called to worship and begin their act of praise as those called before God's Word. Whenever we cross the threshold of a church and share in an act of worship, we enter a world of symbols – a world in which words, bodily actions, artefacts and the very fabric of the building, its arrangement and furnishing, carries a freight of symbolic meaning. As we press towards a clarification of the notion of symbols and to a greater appreciation of the symbolic dimension of worship, we need to recognize the ways in which symbols and symbolic actions can carry and convey meaning. Our first step could well be quite pragmatic as we register these ways that symbols are used in worship.

There is merit in this approach and its simplicity is commendable, especially if our primary concern is to engage the attention of worshippers and stage our worship in an imaginative and creative way. A recent booklet has taken this approach (Leach 2005) but reflecting on the specific examples described in it I was left with the question of whether the author had limited symbols to striking visual aids for prayer and worship. The message that we need to attend to the visual dimension of worship and seek to engage the senses of worshippers in an act of worship is certainly welcome, but the danger of limiting the symbols to visual aids and a means of enhancing the ambience of the worship space is similar to the use of vivid illustrations in preaching when the hearer remembers the illustrations but fails to grasp the content of the preacher's message. To draw a cultural parallel, we might recall how the most effective advertising operates in the most subtle and even subliminal way, and by comparison much church-sponsored communication and image-making can seem second-rate, if not a little naïve and simplistic. A notorious example was the 1995 Church of England-sponsored Easter advert, devoid of traditional reference, which simply said 'Surprise' (Torevell 2000: p. 176). The risk of confusing symbols with visual aids is that we might simply end up dressing banalities and worn clichés in new clothes. The question remains, however, of how we might recover our 'lost icons' (Williams 2000) and deepen our appreciation of the full meaning of symbols.

The anthropologist Dan Sperber insists that symbols cannot simply be equated with language, and he questions whether a symbol can be adequately accounted for in terms of semantic meaning. Symbols undoubtedly play a key role in human communication and, as Sperber seems to suggest, the very process of symbolization functions as the 'information processor' of the human mind. But do symbols actually tell us anything and contribute to our knowledge of God, ourselves and the world around us? Do they, in short, have a cognitive function and contribute to our knowledge? These are rather fundamental questions and have certainly been addressed by Christian thinkers and writers from earliest times. The so-called Apologists of the second century, for instance, rigorously defended the place of Christianity in a sophisticated world. Even the cross of Christ, the most ubiquitous sign of God's salvation, was stamped into the very structures of the physical world, they claimed, and was visibly reproduced in human artefacts, such as the mast of the sailing ship. Wherever one looked, one was struck by the sign of the cross.

Bishop Irenaeus of Lyons claimed that as God was the creator of all things, so there was nothing in the created world which did not signify God. Presumably what Irenaeus is saying here presupposes an analogical relationship between the creation and its creator, enabling us to read something of God's will and power in the elements of the physical world. This was certainly the view taken up and developed in subsequent theological reflection. Maximus the Confessor (580–662) argued that our very knowledge of God and of divine realities was mediated through symbols (from the Greek word *sym-balein*, 'to put together, side by side'), and that our knowledge widened, and indeed deepened, when we came to recognize spiritual significance in those material things which are perceived through the senses. On this basis, Maximus insists, such growth in the knowledge of divine realities amounts to wisdom, the capacity to apprehend the presence and action of God through our experience of sensible phenomena. Building on the earlier work of Augustine of Hippo, Thomas Aquinas said something similar. Augustine had already established the premise that the reading of signs (from the Latin word *signum*) progressively 'leads to knowledge of something other than itself' (*De doctrina Christiana* 2). Aquinas, again writing in Latin, argued that in reading what he refers to as 'sensible signs' we can progress from what is known to what is unknown, from what is seen to what is unseen, in a spiral of knowledge from the sensual to the spiritual.

Signs and symbols

What this brief survey demonstrates is a convergence within our theological sources. Both those who wrote in Greek and used the word 'symbol', and those who wrote in the more terse and economical language of Latin and used the term 'sign', argued that symbols played a significant part in our putting together (as in a jigsaw puzzle) our picture of the world and in our coming to understand God and the playing out of the divine purpose in human lives and in the created order. In this sense, symbols do have a cognitive function. They not only open the doors of our perception so that we might grasp that which is beyond what immediately strikes the eye, but also draw us into a deeper apprehension of 'the deep-down things', of what is really real. In our own terms, this Christian understanding affirms what we would call the communicative power and cognitive function of signs and symbols. Such an understanding is, perhaps predictably, heightened by contemporary writers from Orthodox and Roman Catholic traditions (e.g. Schmemann 1987 and Chauvet 1995, respectively), but it is interesting to see this matter treated in the work of John McIntyre. McIntyre, writing from a Reformed perspective on how we might articulate a sense of God in the context of contemporary culture (McIntyre 1997), argued that our very use of symbols is itself a way of knowing, and that symbols give access to the reality they symbolize. In his understanding, the symbols with which we deal in the practice of our religious life are not clues we need to search for, nor indeed things we might manufacture for ourselves, but things which are God-given. As he reminds us, God gives us the rainbow in the sky as a *sign* (Hebrew *'oth*) that he will not devastate and destroy his creation (Genesis 9.12), and looking towards that more perfect and complete symbol, the Christ who holds together in his person the fully human and the truly divine, we might also recall the sign offered to the prophet Isaiah, that a young woman would conceive and bear a son (Isaiah 7.14). In these cases the 'sign' operates in a way which exceeds a reminder, an emblem or a token, and actualizes the very promises of God and opens finite reality up to the transcendent in the present. This dynamic conception of 'sign' is certainly one which we might well carry forward as we seek to construct a more adequate understanding of the Christian sacramental actions of baptismal washing, anointing, and eucharistic eating and drinking.

However, we must not anticipate the discussion that is to come, but remain with the analytical question as to whether and to what extent it is possible to differentiate between sign and symbol. We have already noted that some difference between sign and symbol can be traced back to their respective language roots, namely Latin and Greek respectively. Even so, there are instances when the term 'sign' seems to operate in the same way as 'symbol' and in the end we must reckon that there is an element of sign in the symbol and an element of symbol in the sign.

The fact is that in the writings of theoreticians, both philosophers and theologians, we stumble upon contradictory definitions. What one writer says about the nature and function of signs, another will say about symbols and vice versa.

Although the attempt to differentiate between signs and symbols is admittedly problematic, it is possible to sketch some general characteristics and draw some distinctions. If one's measure is precision and directness of communication, then it is the sign that ranks first. The way we ordinarily speak about symbols is that they are vague, imprecise. 'It's only a symbol', we might say, suggesting that what we really prize is precision in communication. The German philosopher Ernst Cassirer, whose work was developed and applied to the arts by Susanne Langer, tried to counterbalance such a positivist approach and argued that the human story of the making of meaning was also a symbolic enterprise as we sought not only to describe but also evoke (and indeed invoke) the forces that shape our lives and inform our deepest feelings. Human language itself is not only descriptive and explanatory, but also expressive and suggestive. Cassirer did not want to oppose these two functions of language, but wanted to highlight the role of symbols, particularly in the myths we spin to convey our values and ideologies, both religious and political. The depth psychologist Carl Jung was fascinated by dreams as well as myths, and explored what he saw as the frequent concurrence of symbols between the two phenomena. For Jung a 'symbol' was characterized by its wide connotation (1979: pp. 4–8). Similarly both Victor Turner and Paul Ricœur spoke of 'condensed symbols', thus highlighting how symbols are polyvalent, and able to carry a multiplicity of meanings which appeal to the mind, the memory, our feelings, and pre-eminently the imagination.

In contrast to the wide connotation and multivalency of the symbol, particularly a natural symbol such as water, which can trigger and combine a range of different and even contradictory associations, memories, relations and feelings, the 'sign' is often taken as having a precise denotation. A sign, such as a road sign, points to the reality it indicates, and in pointing to what it refers to relates to that thing (person or event) as an object. What it refers to, in other words, is something other than itself, and it refers specifically to that designated thing and not to any other thing, or relation. In semiotic terms, a direct link is posited between the signifier (the sign) and the signified (the thing or state of affairs it points to), and what it conventionally points to it simply points to, and to the exclusion of anything else. So the sign, unlike the symbol, is specific in its denotation, and as it operates as a pointer to something else, it cannot stand in the place of that to which it points, or mediate the reality of that to which it refers. It is neither expressive nor invocative, but is deliberately designed to transmit information, and to do so unambiguously and as efficiently as possible.

Even more precise than signs are signals. On hearing the sound of a fire alarm, we realize we should evacuate the building immediately. The sight of a flashing blue light in a driver's rearview mirror signals to the driver that he or she should pull in to allow an emergency vehicle to pass. Again, when the traffic signal turns red we must stop immediately. In this case, the visual signal requires a precise and learnt behavioural response. For this to happen, these signs and signals have to be authorized by what is considered to be a competent public body. By being authorized by a competent public agency and socially agreed, signs are known as conventional signs, and are therefore in one sense quite arbitrary. But not all signs are of this type. We might also consider natural signs, like dark clouds being a sign of rain, and draw a distinction between something being a 'sign for' and, in the latter case, a 'sign of'. In the first case, the sign simply refers to something else, whereas the second does not necessarily deliver what is presaged in the sign, i.e. the cloud might pass without it raining. So in both cases, there is no intrinsic connection between the sign and what is signified.

Conventional signs are fixed and deliberately designed to convey specific information, but this does not mean that they cannot be misread, or misconstrued. The sign placed by a cleaner outside a public convenience is a cautionary sign signalling a wet floor, not advertising a skating rink. This rather facile observation brings us back to the point that conventional signs are functional and serve a utilitarian purpose. They are invented and we have to learn what they mean. In this sense they are socially invented and marketed constructs. A recent example is the red ribbon used as an emblem to be worn on World Aids Day. In this case, the publicity campaign has been such so international that the sign is now ubiquitous. As signs are generally utilitarian, deliberately designed to convey a specific and practical piece of information, they are often ranked higher than symbols, which are often taken to be less precise, and therefore less reliable in transmitting the message we seek to communicate.

The high premium placed on information technology in western societies undoubtedly adds to the problem of securing a more positive estimate of the place and value of symbols, as distinct from signs. A further reflection illustrates how these cultural assumptions influence the sphere of Christian worship. A worshipping community cannot remove itself from the cultural assumptions of the society in which it is set, and in an increasingly utilitarian society whatever 'gets the message across' will inevitably be more highly prized than those things which are communicated through a more complex system of symbols. One is already hearing claims that in practice a multi-media presentation might be more effective in Christian 'mission' than the inaccessible symbolism of sacramental worship. Every area and activity in contemporary life, from education to health care, is now measured by the question of whether it 'delivers the goods'. The index of value is not so much the quality of what a thing is, but its outcome, and whether it functions efficiently. In this prevailing utilitarian view of the world the question of what something is worth is determined by its practical usefulness and economic efficiency. The engine of a consumer society is finance, the economic mechanism of 'getting and spending', and in the wider social scene it is interesting to observe how some cultural symbols, such as the Easter egg, have been appropriated in such a way as to remove them from any religious context and connotation, and convert them into a seasonal economic currency. In this instance, the Easter egg, removed from a religious association, is reduced to a sign signifying a huge consumer and marketing enterprise. But when we look to the realm of personal relationships and aesthetic and religious experience, there might well be some things whose practical usefulness or economic value is not immediately obvious, nor, indeed, relevant.

Such cultural factors add impetus to the task of seeking to elucidate the meaning of signs and symbols. As we have indicated, the meaning of a sign, even the most perfectly designed visual emblem, is not always transparent, and similarly, a conventional religious symbol seems both to reveal and to conceal what it mediates at one and the same time. A shadow, we might say, invariably falls between the signifier and the thing signified. We have already said that a sign is indicative, a pointing to something else, which presupposes a distance between the signifier and the signified. The one may indeed correspond to the other, but it is not commensurate with it, and cannot be identified with the reality to which it points. And this distance between sign and signified must have some bearing on how we might construe 'sacramental signs'. Working with the classic definition of sacraments as 'effective signs', as signs that effect what they signify, we also need to reckon with the distance between the signifier and the signified. In terms of the eucharistic gifts, for instance, this aspect of the function of a sign might help us to grasp how Christ can be both sacramentally present, and yet 'elsewhere' as the ascended Lord of all. But an adequate description of a 'sacramental sign' requires something more to be said beyond the assertion that a sacrament *focuses* for us a sense of presence. Indeed, as we try and see how Christ might be present, of how he 'makes himself known in the breaking of bread', we find ourselves shifting our ground from the language of signs to that of symbols. That is, we move away from the kind of representation belonging to signs to a real personal connection or communion with what is symbolized. We might recall that the recognition on the part of the two disciples in Luke's story of the encounter

11

at Emmaus occurs in the process of symbolization, in the very ritual act of the Word and the 'breaking of bread'.

Showing and making present

The point here is that symbols involve the communicating self, and bear upon and make claims upon the subject, whereas signs belong to an objective system of direct communication. So we might place signs in the sphere of information, and symbol in the realm of personal interaction, and it is precisely within this locus of ritual *action* that a sacramental sign becomes a symbol. In performing the action the sacramental sign operates as a real symbol, for what is designated in sign becomes present, and what is intended becomes a reality. To explicate this further we might reflect on what is happening in the context in which we hear these words spoken: 'I sign you with the sign of the cross', and 'With this ring, I thee wed'. They are examples of what have come to be known as 'performative utterances', for in the saying of these words something happens beyond the physical act of speech. In saying these sorts of things we are doing something, and what is done in such cases alters the standing of the speaker. And as it is with some kinds of speech, so it is with symbols in worship. For what we see in this case are generally symbolic actions, such as washing with water, lighting a candle, eating bread and drinking wine, and as we 'do' something in speech, so in our symbolic actions something happens. As Louis-Marie Chauvet neatly put it, in liturgy we do what we say, and what is done in the liturgy has immediate bearing on our relationships with each other and to God and affects our very sense of identity (Chauvet 1995: pp. 326–9). We shall later return to this point of locating the power of symbols in their performance, but first let us return to the story of the encounter on the road to Emmaus and see if there is another clue here as to how we might further differentiate between signs and symbols.

There is a feature in this post-resurrection narrative, as in the Last Supper narratives, which again draws us away from the arbitrary or invented character of signs to that of symbols, and that is the 'given' aspect of the symbol, which incidentally is implicit in Ricœur's maxim 'the symbol gives rise to thought' (see Ricœur 1967: p. 348). Jesus took bread, broke it . . . and *gave* it to them. On the face of it this is a reported historic fact, but the question of eucharistic food and drink is a contested question. We might say that the use of bread and wine is established by custom, but if we understand the eucharistic gifts in terms of signs, then the elements themselves take on a more arbitrary quality and there is greater scope for using food and drink that is more culturally appropriate, such as tortillas in Spain and rice wine in Japan. If on the other hand we see the elements more in terms of symbols, then the ground rules of our discourse subtly change. Signs are in one sense invented, constructed as well as agreed. With symbols there is the sense of something being 'given', not only in terms of what is historically given and established by custom, but also in terms of how these symbols echo the complex web of scriptural imagery and actually work on the human psyche and, in Turner's understanding (1967: ch. 4) our social processes. The element of the 'givenness' of the symbol, at least in part, might underline what the German Reformer Martin Luther meant when he insisted that even the Church cannot institute a sacrament, but this again points to the multiple meanings which a symbol might carry. This multivalency, which is often assigned as a defining characteristic of symbols, can be accounted for in these three ways:

1 How a given symbol connects with the nexus of biblical images;
2 How it resonates with the diverse range of our (conscious and unconscious) experience, even holding together contradictory experience, as in the case of the natural symbol of water, which is both vivifying and destructive; and
3 How, in the range of evocation covered in points 1 and 2, the symbol engages our emotions, will and affections.

In what has become a classic discussion of the nature and importance of symbols in religious discourse and practice, the

German-American Protestant theologian Paul Tillich drew attention to the ways in which what are first established as signs can
come, presumably through their placing and repeated usage, to
assume symbolic significance (Tillich 1959: p. 65). A more recent
study of church art and architecture has again highlighted how
the placing of artefacts in the spatial layout of a church building
can add to their symbolic significance (Seasoltz 2005). Among
this category of 'sign-symbols' one might also include such things
as the altar, a sign of the presence of Christ in the midst of the
community, and the *cathedra*, the designated seat of the bishop
as a sign of the continuity of the apostolic teaching within an
ordered, as distinct from an *ad hoc*, community being a part of
the wider, universal Church. On the other hand, symbols can also
slide across the scale and become signs, traces of a largely for-
gotten religious belief and practice. Arguably, this might be the
case for the crucifix, as we recall the story of the young person
asking a jeweller for one of 'those crosses with a little man on it'.
But it is not simply a question of religious symbols dying because
of the increasing secularization in our consumer society. Indeed,
we might also contribute to the muting of symbols within the
Church by that irresistible urge of some clergy to offer a commentary on all that is seen and done during an act of worship.
What I would affirm is that symbols have an eloquence of their
own and we should allow them to 'speak'. Further, we should also
recognize that what keeps symbols 'alive' are the communities which
use and handle them in sensitive and imaginative ways, a point
which neatly returns us to our account of liturgical symbols.

The symbol (whether of an event, a person or an object),
unlike a fixed sign, is dynamic and manifests or mediates something of the reality of what it is that it symbolizes. I would not
claim that the dynamism of the symbol is intrinsic to the nature
of the element, but rather point to how it is placed and handled
in the performance of a religious rite, that is, to its context. This
point is heightened, if not exaggerated, by the Catholic sacramental
theologian Crispino Valenziano, who insists that we must take the
term 'symbol' as a verb, an action word, and not a noun or a name

(Chupungco 1998: p. 34). To put it another way, we might say that the 'power of symbols' is to be seen in how and where they are placed, and the context in which their use constitutes an essential aspect of the whole realm of discourse, with its exchange of words, objects and actions. Indeed, we could say that once a symbol is removed from the context of a symbolic action, it risks becoming a bare sign, a mere reminder of something or someone else, an indicator not of presence, but of an absence. For a symbol only becomes a living symbol within actual exchange and communicative acts between people, and crucially, when it is regarded and responded to in an intentional way. Such an understanding returns us to the etymology of the term and can be illustrated by the following example. Imagine the breaking of a terracotta pot, and a shard being given to each person who witnessed the event. The group disperses, but each person knows that the piece of pottery they possess, though an individual fragment, binds them in some way to the whole group. A symbol, as we have said, joins and holds us together, and if we are disposed to respond to it, our sense of being connected, of being bound together, becomes a living and affective bond. In this regard, we might recall how St Paul speaks of the mystery of the Eucharist and our being made one body in Christ: 'though we are many, we are one body, because we all share in the one bread' (1 Corinthians 10.17f.).

Liturgical symbols, or symbolization

What we are saying is that religious symbols come alive in the very symbolic act, in the performance of an actual rite. But this is not to say that the symbolic exchange is complete simply in its performance (that would be tantamount to magic), for the symbol also needs to be received and responded to. The point was well made by artist Mark Rothko, who said that a painting could only come 'alive' when it was viewed by a sensitive viewer responding to its form and colour. Religiously speaking, some might say that this is the point at which faith comes into play in the symbolic exchange of Christian worship. Indeed, without the appropriate intention, attention and receptivity on the part of worshippers in the symbolic exchange of worship, the symbol is in danger of becoming a mere empty sign. But this is not to say that the power of a symbol resides in what we, the participants, attribute to or invest in the material symbol. On the contrary, a vital element of what is said and done in an act of worship is the element of *invocation*, specifically, the invocation of the Holy Spirit that we ourselves may be changed by the symbolic exchange of such physical things as bread and wine, ash, light, water and oil in the context of an actual liturgical celebration (see Irvine 2005: ch. 5). The Reformer John Calvin had no hesitation is speaking of the Eucharist as a 'symbol', an effective sign that was charged with the Spirit, the life and energies of God, so that in sharing the eucharistic bread and cup, what Christ offers and gives, and what we receive, is his body and blood. Again, as Chauvet has argued at length, sacramental symbols mediate between God and humanity and are experienced as grace, as relationships are reconfigured within the Body and we receive our identity as brothers and sisters in Christ (Chauvet 1995: p. 152ff.).

To reiterate, what we are saying is that it is in the actual celebration, the very doing of worship, that the voice and power of a symbol is realized and released. In the traditional nomenclature, the sacramental symbol is a 'visible sign of invisible grace', effecting what it signifies and revealing the transcendent signifier. And so, what is placed into our hands at Holy Communion is not 'ordinary food', but the Bread of Life. It is in the performance of ritual action that its signs gain or reveal symbolic significance, and for this reason, our full attention must be given to our symbolic practice, of how we use symbols in a liturgical context. For this reason the rest of this Guide will look at the very practical matter of how we place and handle symbols in the celebration of the Church's rites. But having arrived at this point in our enquiry we need to recognize that there are two possibly competing lines of argument regarding the use of symbols in worship. The one, seeking to heighten our sense of the symbolic, urges us to streamline the use of symbols, to free them from all secondary symbolism and distracting clutter or decoration. This we might call the minimalist approach, with its call for uncluttered sanctuaries and unfussy ceremonial and a generous and expansive use of symbols and symbolic actions. The other, the Roman Catholic revisionist position, presses the case that such streamlining of symbolism has actually resulted in the loss of symbols (for this view, see Caldecott 1998 and Torevell 2000).

It is undoubtedly the case that religious symbols attract further symbols, so for instance we find eucharistic vestments decorated with images of eucharistic vessels, or Easter fires that are so large that they dwarf the symbolism of the Easter candle. Symbols and emblems can be layered upon other signs and symbols, rather like barnacles on the surface of a boat's hull. Thomas Merton wrote astringently about this danger in an essay aptly called 'Absurdity in Sacred Decoration' (Merton 1960: pp. 264–73). Merton protested against the obscuring of religious symbols through the multiplication of decorative signs and emblems, but his underlying motive was to highlight the need for religious symbols to be placed and handled in ways which drew and held the focused attention of the worshipper. Such an agenda was rigorously advocated by Balthasar Fischer, who argued that the streamlining of symbols in the wake of liturgical reform, and the recovery of those focal points of liturgical space and furnishing resulting from the liturgical reform after the Second Vatican Council, led to a clearer appreciation of the symbolic dimension of worship (Stevenson 1982: pp. 122–33). Bringing the symbols of worship into greater focus has led not only to a greater appreciation of the need for the visibility of symbols, but also for more expansive symbolic gestures and a lavish use of material symbols. Oil is no longer to be kept in a small silver phial and applied with a piece of cotton wool, but in a large glass decanter to be literally poured over the person being anointed. Similarly, out go the fonts on the scale of a bird bath, and in come the fonts with running water. God's grace is abundant and overflowing and, so the logic goes, our symbolic objects and actions need to be more capacious and more generous. But an extravagant play of symbols is not without proper restraints. As Chauvet reminds us, the ancient people of God were bound to him in a covenant through the sprinkling of blood, that we might taste the Messianic banquet without being satiated, and so a small amount (as long as it is not so small as to slip into insignificance) is sufficient (Chauvet 1995: pp. 346–7; Chauvet 2001: pp. 72–3). In sacramental terms, anyway, a little is a token of much, a 'down payment' of an eschatological (i.e. the 'not yet') abundance, of the *excess* of divine grace.

Coming to understand the place of symbols in worship is not a matter of cracking a code, but simply of opening ourselves to the power of symbol, of allowing ourselves to be drawn into that wondrous exchange where physical actions and objects become expressions of spiritual realities in the wondrous playfulness of the liturgy, through bodily action and the physical elements of God's good creation. So, returning to our opening remarks on contemporary culture, I would argue that liturgical symbols are not simply visual aids, or a means of setting a mood, as, for instance, we might light candles around a bath to create a relaxing atmosphere. Neither do we need to claim any intrinsic power for natural symbols, but instead point primarily to their *use*, and the ritual context in which they are used. This is where I would locate the power of symbols. Further, I would highlight the way in which symbols are evocative, and argue with Victor Turner that within a historically defined social community, symbols and our symbolic actions can carry a freight of multiple meanings (see Turner *The Anthropology of Performance* and *From Ritual to Theater*). When used in the context of worship, symbols can function as the currency of the commerce between the human and divine, the creator and creation, and both mediate and bring to expression God's redeeming engagement with the world, and elicit our response. In conclusion, I would say that liturgical symbols are not simply one element among many in the panoply of worship, but a key mode in which the interaction between the triune God and his people actually occurs.

2

Water

CHRISTOPHER IRVINE

In a striking poem, '*Water*', Philip Larkin said that if he were to invent a religion it would make copious use of water in a variety of ways. Water is universally one of the most frequently used elements in religious ceremonial and ritual action, such as libations and cleansing rituals. The ancient Jewish religion had an acute sense of the holy and of how what was holy could be polluted and contaminated by what was impure. There were strict regulations in the holiness code about diet, the preparation of food, clothing, cleansing rituals, and healing and purification (e.g. Leviticus 11.24–40; 14.5–9; 15.13; Numbers 19). In Jewish practice the ritual use of water was abundant, and the volume of water required is indicated by the reference to the six stone jars of water for purification referred to in John 2.6, which apparently would have held over 120 gallons of water. The first-century ascetic Essene community, who withdrew into the desert at Qumran to prepare for the expected vindication of God's 'righteous ones', practised a repeated ceremonial washing of the body.

In the Diaspora, those Jewish communities in the Roman world outside of Palestine, Gentile converts to Judaism were required to bathe as part of their initiatory process (a practice which seems to have developed at the same time as Christian baptism). Although cleansing was fundamental to a baptismal washing (see Hebrews 6.2), its prototype for Christians was the baptism of Jesus by John the Baptist in the river Jordan. The Baptist had called the people to be cleansed in preparation for the expected and critical Day of the Lord. In this he took up the prophet's demand that the people should wash themselves and seek a fairer and more just society (see Isaiah 1.16–17; cf. Micah 7.19b), in the hope that God would fulfil his promise to make us more humane and compassionate through water and the Spirit (see Ezekiel 36.25).

The first circle of Jesus' disciples may themselves have practised a ritual of washing by water (see John 4.1–4), but Christian baptism, as such, was the bestowal of a new identity as the children of God, through water and the Spirit. When Jesus emerged from the waters of the Jordan he was shown as the Anointed One (the Christ), the beloved Son of the Father, and as such was destined to enter the deep waters of death (see Mark 10.38; Luke 12.50). In Jewish custom a bride would take a pre-nuptial bath, and this practice gave rise to a view of baptism as the way in which a person came to be 'joined to Christ', suggesting the metaphor of the Church as the Bride of Christ (see Ephesians 5.25–27; cf. Revelation 21.2).

In the Acts of the Apostles (8.36), the Ethiopian asks Philip what is to prevent him from being baptized. The sole requirement was the element of water. In the natural world, there can be no life without water. The multiple religious uses of water, as we will see, build on the natural qualities of water and the ways in which we use it in hygiene, to slake our thirst, to irrigate our gardens and nurture our crops. In addition the symbol of water also connects with a range of scriptural images and stories which tell of God's work of making and remaking his creation and in calling people to be his own. The biblical story begins with a reference to the four rivers flowing through Paradise (Genesis 2.10–14), and ends with a vision of the river of the water of life (Revelation 22.1). In between, watery incidents occur as the narrative of salvation unfolds. Noah and his family are saved from the destroying waters in the ark (Genesis 7.6–23). The infant Moses is rescued and adopted by Pharaoh's daughter from the waters of the Nile (Exodus 2.1–10). The people of God are liberated from their bondage through the waters of the Red Sea, and enter the land of promise across the water of the river Jordan. The saving figures

Moses, for Israel, and Christ, for followers of the Way, are presented as providers of water. During the time of Israel's desert wandering, Moses splits open the rock that they might drink of the water (Exodus 17.2–7; Numbers 20.10–11), and in his encounter with the woman at the well, Christ reveals himself as the 'living water' (John 4.10; cf. 1 Corinthians 10.4), in whom our thirst for God is satisfied, and through whom healing is given (see John 5.2; cf. 9.6–7) and the promise of the Spirit is made (John 7.37–39).

Unsurprisingly then, in the place where these stories are rehearsed and heard, the element of water evokes and resonates with a range of images, associations and meanings. And because these associations converge upon the paradoxical life-giving and life-destroying features of water, that element holds together (*symbolein*) life and death, and connects nature and Spirit, gospel and creation. Water is the primary and most potent symbol in Christian life and worship. But how can the simple physical element of water be charged with such significance?

In the Old Testament Naaman the leper expressed some consternation at being asked simply to bathe in the Jordan seven times (2 Kings 5.11), and Tertullian in his treatise on baptism (AD 200) acknowledged that to think washing in water could achieve all that is claimed to happen in baptism defied all logic (*De Baptismo* 2.1). But as John Chrysostom put it so long ago: 'Some might think that baptism is nothing but water, no more than a washing of the body, but we think of the tomb, of the resurrection, of sanctification and redemption and the adoption as sons of our heavenly inheritance, of the Kingdom of heaven and the gift of the Holy Spirit.' The basis on which we can predicate such a web of significance is the *context*, in the sense of both the setting and what happens there, and texts belonging to the community that gathers there. The texts which are read and heard by the Christian community tell of a whole constellation of biblical events associated with water, freighting the element with multiple meanings. These meanings are triggered and brought into consciousness most forcefully by the use of water in our ritual practice, in the actual *doing* of worship, and it is this that we will explore, beginning with the current *Common Worship* provision to mark time in our daily prayer.

Common Worship: Daily Prayer and A Service of the Word

In the *Common Worship* (*CW*) provision for Sunday morning and evening prayer we might particularly note three features. First, the biblical imagery in the optional thanksgiving prayer at the end of the preparation section of Morning Prayer (p. 32) invokes both creation from the waters of chaos, and baptism as new birth through the deep waters of death. Second, there is provision for a Thanksgiving for Holy Baptism (pp. 48–9) drawn from one of the four optional thanksgivings in *Celebrating Common Prayer* (pp. 338–9). This might follow the sermon and involve some movement to the font, presupposing that the font is a sizeable fixture, prominently sited in the architectural space of the church building.

Finally, *Common Worship: Daily Prayer* also provides a form for the Corporate Renewal of Baptismal Vows. This form, and how and when it might be celebrated, will be addressed later in this chapter, but perhaps some preliminary remarks would be useful at this stage of the discussion.

Both the Church of England's Liturgical Commission's Commentary and Notes in *Common Worship: Christian Initiation* (*CI*) reprinted from the earlier *Common Worship: Initiation Services* (*IS*), make it clear that the sacrament of baptism is unrepeatable and can only be administered once. The report *On the Way* endorsed the warning made in the ecumenical Lima document, *Baptism, Eucharist and Ministry*, that any ritual practice that might be interpreted as re-baptism should be avoided, which (contra Buchanan 1993) would preclude any arrangement where an individual stood in, or was submerged in, water for the renewal of promises and an affirmation of faith. Rather than collude with the modernist assumption that what is paramount is the individual and his or her experience (or more likely in this case, providing an experience that the individual feels they have previously missed out on), the challenge is to give baptism a higher priority in the liturgical life, teaching and preaching of the local church and to recover the *social* aspect of baptism as our incorporation into the Body of Christ. Although provision was made in the 1662 Book of Common Prayer for the baptism of infants in a domestic setting (Private Baptism), the evident preference, stated more forcefully in subsequent reports and revisions, is that baptism should be celebrated at a public gathering, preferably in the context of Sunday worship, for the specific reason that members of the congregation might remember their own baptism. The implication of this emphasis on the public performance of the rite is that it is the highly symbolic ritual action of baptism (together with the interactions between those gathered for the celebration) that constitutes the bedrock underlying all our understandings and expressions of Christian life and ministry. So, it is to the service of Holy Baptism that we must now turn.

Common Worship: Holy Baptism

When the baptismal party candidates, their sponsors and families have gathered at the baptismal font, the Prayer of Thanksgiving Over the Water is offered as the president stands before the water. The text of this prayer for general use makes reference to the natural symbolism of water to 'sustain, cleanse and refresh us' and includes three symbols of salvation history: the Spirit hovering over the water at creation, the Exodus through the Red Sea, and the baptism of Jesus by John in the river Jordan. The additional seasonal prayers of thanksgiving focus on other images of salvation. The Easter/Pentecost thanksgiving refers to 'the deep waters of death' (*CI*, p. 158). The seasonal prayer for Epiphany/the Baptism of Christ/Trinity speaks of our sin being drowned in the water of judgement (p. 152), and the All Saints seasonal prayer refers to Noah and deliverance from the 'waters of destruction' (p. 163). One classic motif that is omitted in the *Common*

Worship provision (even in the additional seasonal material for Easter) is the reference to the blood and water flowing from the pierced side of the crucified Christ (John 19.34). The intended meaning of this passage might well have been to draw attention to the reality of Christ's death, but the way it has been received and used has drawn out other meanings from this richly symbolic Johannine statement. Both Augustine and John Chrysostom had no qualms in reversing the scriptural sequence of blood and water, to correspond more exactly to the sacramental sequence of baptism and Eucharist. This association of baptism with Christ's passion heightens the sense of the baptismal water as a laver of divine forgiveness, and it is this sense that is expressed in the prayer immediately before the actual washing by water in the 1662 baptism service, and in George Herbert's 'Holy Baptism (1)'. The omission of this trope (included in contemporary Roman Catholic and Lutheran font blessings) inevitably weakens the rich nexus of symbolic association between baptismal water and the forgiveness of sins and penitence.

An analysis of the structure of the *CW* default prayer of thanksgiving over the water shows how the praying assembly is involved in God's drama of creation and redemption, and is written into the story of God's salvation in its very enactment, as indicated by the repeated use of the first person plural 'we', explicitly linking members of the praying community with the events for which thanks are being offered. It is as though the saving significance of those past watery incidents surface in the present.

The blessing of water for baptism dates back to very early Christian practice and is included in Basil of Caesarea's catalogue of Christian practices which, though not mentioned in scripture, were established by apostolic tradition (*On the Holy Spirit* 27.66). Thus the prayer over the font has generally included a petition for the blessing or sanctification of the water by the Holy Spirit. The phrase 'sanctify this Water to the mystical washing away of sin' was inserted in the 1662 Book of Common Prayer, and the petition in the *Alternative Service Book* (1980) was 'Bless this water, that your servants who are washed in it may be made one with Christ in his death and resurrection.' The *CW* Thanksgiving Prayer Over the Water for general use follows Anglican precedent in maintaining a teleological sense of blessing, namely, the setting apart of something for the specified divine purpose – in this instance, water, specifically for cleansing, regeneration and the renewal of the *imago dei* in those being baptized. Although some voices in Anglican history have objected to the blessing of natural elements and inanimate objects, the blessing of water for baptism has persisted in our authorized services. The general consensus rests in the hope that the Spirit may be operative in those undergoing this ritual act of washing (cf. Titus 3.5).

The celebration of baptism

The actual act of baptism is by immersion (or more quaintly 'dipping'), or by pouring of water over the head of the candidate. The rubric indicates a preference for immersion: 'The president or another minister dips each candidate in water, or pours water on them' (*CI*, p. 71). The presumption here is that the act of baptism (from a Greek verb, *baptizo*, literally meaning 'to drench') requires a copious amount of water. And so, Note 12 on the Administration of Water in *Christian Initiation* states that 'The use of a substantial amount of water is desirable' (p. 100). How might this happen in an actual celebration of baptism?

Some water (of a suitable temperature) can be poured into the font immediately before the service, and in addition, a large stone jar containing water can also be prepared beforehand, placed conveniently on the chancel step, and then carried by a member of the baptism party to the font after the Decision and Signing of the Cross. The essay in the *Companion to Common Worship* also suggests carrying an icon of the baptism of Christ in the procession to the font, as well as the Paschal candle (Bradshaw 2001: p. 167), but the focus should be on the element of water, and in order for the symbolic action to have its full impact upon the congregation, it needs to be a visual and aural symbol as well as a tactile one. So, once the minister has reached the font and all are gathered around it, or at least facing it, the water should be poured into the font in such a way that all may both hear and see the element of flowing water. A similarly generous gesture is required if the candidate is to be baptized by affusion, with a liberal volume of water being poured over the candidate in the administration of the sacramental washing.

The ritual action depends on the quantity of water, which in turn relates to the size of the font. As previously indicated, the English Prayer Books commended 'dipping', thereby marking a point of continuity with established medieval practice, and implying a critique of the small pedestal fonts and the minimalist baptism by sprinkling with water which became popular from the time of the Renaissance. Dipping seems to have been universal practice in both East and West. In the West the baby was lowered into the water horizontally, belly down, as illustrated in a fifteenth-century painting of the baptism of St Ursula, and dunked in the water. In the East, the infants were plunged vertically, feet first. Such historical pictures seem ironic, as we recall how children are advised for their safety not to play too near water. It is a dangerous and ambiguous element. It can both wreak havoc as a tsunami, and provide the protective environment for a foetus in the womb. Some of the early Christian preachers such as Zeno, the early fourth-century bishop of Verona, played on this ambiguity to convey to his hearers the life-giving quality of the baptismal flood in a paradoxical way. An unseen current may take the unsuspecting swimmer under the water and 'cast the person up drowned', but the baptismal water 'receives the dead and casts them up alive' (Jeanes 1995: p. 85; cf. Ephesians 2.1).

Note 12 on the Administration of Water continues with the statement that 'water must at least flow on the skin of the candidate' (p. 100). This phrasing is wonderfully ambiguous, and in the case of infants, one wonders whether it was envisaged that the candidate for baptism should be stripped and baptized naked. Bryan Spinks concludes his recent two-volume study on baptism with a forceful remark that, given our heated churches, there is no excuse not to strip and dip infants into the font (Spinks, *Reformation and Modern Rituals*, p. 211). The stripping and re-clothing of the candidate for baptism certainly has precedents in primitive practice, and the ritual action of being clothed after the washing in water (as provided for in *Common Worship*) is an eloquent way of symbolizing that aspect of baptism enunciated by St Paul as the stripping off of the old Adam and 'putting on Christ' (Galatians 3.27). Such nakedness also recalls that aspect of baptism as rebirth, as the candidates, rather like the figures of Jonah and Daniel in early Christian art, having been delivered from danger, appear nude as on the day of their birth. Augustine of Hippo (Sermon 376) called the newly baptized, both adults and children, *infants*, for they were 'born anew' (1 Peter 1.3b, 23).

Regarding the actual administering of the baptismal water, again the Notes draw attention to the ancient practice of a three-fold pouring or immersion as a symbolic enactment of our being baptized into the mystery of the Trinity and suggest that an expansive use of the element can vividly bring home to us the meaning of baptism. Historically, the symbolic significance of this practice has varied from region to region. Ambrose of Milan saw the triple immersion as symbolizing Christ's three days in the tomb, and the old Spanish books require a single pouring or immersion in the name of the Trinity, apparently to underline the unity of the triune God (Mitchell 1991: p. 94). The point remains, however, that it is the *use* of water in the baptismal rite which provides the dramatic element to the distinctive and defining moment of our Christian believing and belonging.

The reference in the Notes to a 'substantial amount of water' again bears on the design, setting and indeed, the very size of the font. The place of the font has been a key consideration in the design and reordering of churches and their furnishings. The medieval arrangement was for the font to be sited at the back of the nave near the door, symbolizing the means of entry into the Church. In the design of new churches in the 1960s, when the altar was taken as the focal point from which everything else radiated,

J. G. Davies insisted that the font too should be prominently sited in the architectural space (see Lockett 1964: pp. 1–12). More recently, Richard Giles's reordering of St Thomas's, Huddersfield gives equal and complementary significance to the altar and font along the east/west axis. The choir-wise, arced seating arrangement literally links the twin foci of font and altar. The font is a spacious receptacle and pumps the water in a circular action so that the element literally flows, giving constant sight and sound of water for those who have gathered for worship.

Natural watercourses correspond in our ritual map-making to what the anthropologist styles a *transitus*, or crossing-point, marking a significant change in an individual's status within a community or tribe. In the biblical story one might recall the four rivers marking Paradise, the Red Sea marking the crossing from slavery to freedom, and the Jordan marking the crossing-point to the promised land. The positioning of the font in our churches can also act as a kind of *transitus*, a threshold to be crossed if one's status and place within a community is to be changed. A good example is the placing of the coffin-like cruciform font in Portsmouth Cathedral at the crossing-point under the central tower, between the gathering space of the new nave and the spacious and light choir, where the congregation gather to celebrate the Eucharist. The movement from one architectural space to another literally entails passing by the font, representing a significant threshold or crossing-point. The liturgical template for this reordering is the celebration by the diocesan bishop of baptism and confirmation and Eucharist at the Easter Vigil, a service and a setting for a 'pilgrim people' liturgically enacting their journey of faith. Wherever the font is placed, it needs to be a prominent feature in the architectural space of a church in order to provide a constant and accessible reminder of baptism.

The first Christians undoubtedly baptized converts in convenient natural pools of rivers or streams, and a vestige of this can be seen in early documentary evidence in which a clear preference is expressed for baptism to take place in 'live' or running water, that is in places where water flows (*Didache* 7.1; *Apostolic*

Tradition 22). Interestingly, the baptistery built around 315 by Constantine the Great in Rome, San Giovanni in Fonte, was constructed on the site of a Roman bathhouse, where there was presumably a source of running water. The fourth-century octagonal font in Milan, some 8.5 metres in diameter, seems to have been fed by a natural spring which would have made the water appear 'live'. We do not know exactly how baptism was administered at this site, where allegedly Augustine of Hippo was baptized, but it is likely that the practice was modelled on the early iconography of Christ's baptism, with the adult candidate standing in the water and a triple pouring, or affusion, of water.

Some scholars draw a clear distinction between baptism by immersion and by submersion, argue that submersion involved the candidate being literally plunged under the water, and conclude that this gives the fullest expression to the paschal significance of the rite of Christian initiation. The pattern has been taken up by those Roman Catholic churches influenced by the late twentieth-century Catechumenal Movement, as well as the Roman Catholic staged Rite of Christian Initiation of Adults (RCIA), famously by the Church of Pius V in Pasadena, Texas and the London Roman Catholic churches of Guardian Angels and St Charles Borromeo, where adult candidates enter into a cruciform font sunk into the floor of the building, similar to a baptismal tank in a Baptist church, and are submerged under the water. Anita Stauffer (1994: p. 59) wisely says that this mode of administering baptism should be performed without haste, as gracefully as possible; otherwise, it can easily resemble a ducking in a swimming pool.

There was undoubtedly a variety of practice in the different geographical centres of the early Church, but an outline of how baptism was administered is suggested by archaeological evidence and contemporary catechetical instructions. In some places it seems as though the water in the font came up to the candidate's ankles; in others, such as the fourth-century octagonal font in Poitiers, France, the depth (1.3 metres) would suggest that the water came up to the candidate's waist, and that the Trinitarian confession of faith was followed by a triple immersion. In Milan, Ambrose's sacramental teaching emphasized the identification of the candidate with Christ's death and resurrection. The candidate entered the font from the west and emerged from the east, an orientation that carried its own symbolic significance, first, in representing the dawn of the Sun that never sets, the risen Christ, and second, in recalling the location of the biblical paradise, a garden set in the east. As a ritual enactment, baptism, our being plunged into the paschal mystery of Christ's death and resurrection, is also a *transitus* (literally a 'crossing over'), a transition or 'passing over' from death to life.

Of course, in the mythology of Greek and Roman religions, as well as in later European folklore, gods and spirits, both beneficent and malevolent, have been associated with streams, springs and holy wells. Early Christian iconography of the baptism of Jesus often depicts a personified river god in the water witnessing the epiphany. The association of water and the world of spirits is undoubtedly a significant feature of the religious imagination, and undoubtedly influences religious practice at a deep psychological level (see Lathrop 2003: pp. 62, 67, 94). Early fourth- and fifth-century pilgrims to the Holy Land certainly visited streams and natural water springs associated with holy places and figures. Examining the literary and archaeological evidence, Juliette Day has concluded that bathing in these waters was not associated with baptism as such, but was more akin to ritual washing, and was related to the impulse to take water from a holy place (Day 1999: p. 43). Similar ritual behaviour is seen today, for example, at the well of the Holy House at Walsingham. It is implausible to presume that those pilgrims who take water from a sacred site regard it as having apotropaic powers, or, to be even more pejorative, think of it as 'magic'. The water is significant as a natural symbol of cleansing and refreshment, but its association with a sacred site is probably the decisive factor in how it is used. In the end, the religious use of water evades a full analytical explanation, but as the poet says:

Running water never disappointed.
Crossing water always furthered something.
Stepping stones were stations of the soul.

(Heaney 1991)

The 'breaking of the waters' is the prelude of every natural birth, the releasing of the amniotic fluid as the labour pain reaches its climax. The metaphor of the font as the womb of Mother Church is a commonplace in Patristic preaching and sacramental teaching, and is a dominant image in the writings of those associated with the early Christian centres in Jerusalem, Antioch and elsewhere in Syria. But this maternal imagery was not solely an eastern Christian emphasis. An inscription in the fifth-century Lateran baptistery in Rome speaks of the baptismal water of the 'birth-giving' Church. Unsurprisingly then, the theme of the water's fecundity was soon written into the prayers of the rite. The prayer of blessing of the water in the eighth-century Gelasian Sacramentary invokes the Holy Spirit upon the water in order that the font might be the fruitful womb through which those to be baptized might be reborn as new creatures by water and the Spirit. Such figurative language is rooted in the primary baptismal metaphor of 'rebirth', which we find in the earliest strata of Christian reflection. The key text concerning the need to be reborn of water and the Spirit is in John's Gospel (3.5), and alongside this one might also consider the description of baptism in 1 Peter 1.23, 'You have been born anew', and the very early testimony of Justin Martyr (AD 150), who tells us that those who are led to the water are reborn (*First Apology* 61). Although some recent accounts of baptism seem to regard the so-called Paschal model of baptism and the rebirth model as polar opposites, at root they are inextricably linked. For it is the same Nicodemus to whom Christ addresses his words in John 3 who later in the narrative accompanies Joseph of Arimathaea and prepares the body of Jesus for burial in the tomb. Thus, through the narrative flow of John's Gospel, the baptismal themes of birth and death are united in the single character of

Nicodemus, making it difficult for the reader simply to oppose the Johannine and the Pauline (or, more precisely, Romans 6) readings of baptism.

It is singularly appropriate, then, that we are vividly reminded of baptism at the celebration of the Paschal mystery, the Easter Vigil. In the full-blown language of fourth-century Christian mystagogy (sacramental teaching) we can say that at the baptismal font we are plunged into the Paschal mystery of Christ's death and resurrection and emerge from the womb of Mother Church. Even when there are no actual baptisms, it is customary at the Easter Vigil to invite the congregation to approach the font to recall the very source of their Christian life. The water symbolizes for the Christian community the source of Christian life, and after the Prayer of Thanksgiving Over the Water, individuals approach the water, perhaps making the sign of the cross with it, or just gently splashing their faces. And, as indicated in a rubric in the Easter Liturgy in *Common Worship: Times and Seasons*, hymns and songs may be sung as this unhurried, informal and yet reflective ritual action is taking place. The traditional antiphon provided in the Roman provision is the *Vidi aquam*, drawn from Ezekiel 47: 'I saw water flowing from below the threshold of the temple towards the east, alleluia ...'

In his analysis of aquatic symbolism the anthropologist Mircea Eliade speaks of water as *fons et origo*, the 'spring and origin' of all the possibilities of human existence (Eliade 1959: p. 130), and we can see how this natural element becomes a *condensed* symbol (cf. Turner and Ricœur) as it is used ritually in baptism, attracting to itself a variety of biblical images of fecundity and rebirth. This layering of symbolic significance makes the font more than a mere receptacle for the water; it becomes a symbol in itself. As such, the font is removed from the realm of the utilitarian and comes to be seen not just as a focal point, but also as a mediating symbol of our becoming those who are born of God (cf. John 1.13). In a sermon preached on 'White Sunday', the Sunday after Easter Day, Augustine of Hippo urged those who had been baptized the previous week to return and reverence the font in which they had been baptized, for it was, he impressed upon them, the very fount of their new life in Christ (Sermon 322; PL 38, 1443).

These Eastertide customs return us to the difficult question of the renewal of baptismal promises, and the difficult pastoral scenario of requests by adults baptized as children for 'rebaptism'. The major issues are addressed in the report *On the Way* and in the commentary on *Initiation Services*. The renewal of baptismal promises is a fairly recent innovation, introduced into the Easter Vigil by the Roman Catholic Church in its 1951 revision of Holy Week services. The form was drawn up with the understanding that it was to follow actual baptisms. The Church of England provision for use at the Easter liturgy in *Times and Seasons* is called 'Reaffirmation of Baptismal Vows', and in *Christian Initiation* and *New Patterns for Worship* is called the 'Renewal of Baptismal Vows'. Notwithstanding the language used in the Catechism of the English Prayer Books (1549, 1552, 1662), no 'vows', strictly speaking, are made at baptism, and for this reason 'Renewal of Baptism' might have been a more felicitous expression.

Liturgical forms for the remembrance of baptism, such as the annual *Pascha annotinum*, when families and godparents would bring children to church to give joyful thanksgiving for their baptism and at which prayers were offered for the grace to continue in the life of the baptized, are found in the old liturgical books, and continued to be practised in France until the ninth century. The need for us to 'remember our baptism' was proclaimed by the Reformers Luther and Calvin, and the point has been echoed more recently. Gordon Lathrop, for instance, asserts that baptism takes a lifetime to unfold (Lathrop 2003: p. 115), and Maxwell Johnson concludes his study of the history of baptismal rites with a forceful statement of our need to return again and again to the baptismal waters and to live out of a deeper 'baptismal consciousness' (Johnson 1999: p. 366).

A literal returning to the font is certainly one way of 'remembering baptism', and has precedent in those early liturgical books with provision for an annual commemoration of baptism. It is in this connection that a rubrical note in the *Common Worship* order of baptism and confirmation within Holy Communion, and the order for baptism and confirmation within a Vigil service, allows both for candidates for confirmation, and for those seeking reception within the Church of England, to come forward to the font, after candidates for baptism have been baptized, to sign themselves with the baptismal water, or for it to be sprinkled over them by the presiding bishop. A similar ritual action is allowed, if not encouraged, in the form of service entitled 'Rites of Affirmation' in the raft of Church of England Initiation Services. The point is firmly made in the Liturgical Commission's commentary placed at the end of *Christian Initiation* that these symbolic acts of signing oneself with water, or being sprinkled with it, are to be commended on two grounds. First, they are a strong ritual action, and second, they do not give any appearance of being a second baptism. The point is fairly made that as individuals approach the font to sign themselves with the water, this is a personal act of piety, an act of remembering one's baptism, and so a clear stipulation is made that no words should be used as this ritual act takes place.

Common Worship: Times and Seasons

Reference has already been made to the provision of a form for what is called a Corporate Renewal of Baptismal Vows. The Notes spell out that this form is for occasional use and that it fits particular festival celebrations, specifically Easter, Pentecost, the Baptism of Christ in Epiphany, and particular occasions such as the inauguration of a new ministry, the licensing of a minister, or an induction of an incumbent. In terms of content one might ask whether such a form of service should have focused more on the gifts and graces received in baptism, rather than on the so-called promises that are made by the candidates and their sponsors at an actual baptism, which really are responses to the promises of God. For this reason, the Thanksgiving for Baptism in the Epiphany section of *Times and Seasons* is a very welcome resource, not least in recovering the other ancient season for the celebration of baptism. This well-phrased and well-structured form of thanksgiving for baptism is provided for the Eucharist on the Feast of the Baptism of Christ, the Sunday following the Feast of the Epiphany (6 January). After the sermon, water is taken and poured into the font. A prayer of thanksgiving is uttered over the water and this is followed by prayers of penitence and dedication. Then follows the usual rubric allowing sprinkling, or an invitation to the congregation to approach the water and sign themselves with the cross by it, as the president says: ' "Come", says the Spirit and the Bride; "Come forward you who are thirsty" . . .'

Further provision, a Service for the Festival of the Baptism of Christ (adapted from *The Promise of His Glory*) stands alone as a service of the Word, or as an element in an Epiphany Vigil service, an Epiphany procession or a carol service, and also makes use of the symbol of water. Again water is taken in procession to the font. A thanksgiving prayer, which echoes the form of the eastern Byzantine rite, is recited over the water, and the direction is given that the water may be sprinkled over the people, or placed in vessels by the door for them to make the sign of the cross thereby or, the final and most surprising option, poured out over the threshold. An optional versicle and response, 'Remember your baptism, into Christ Jesus. **Thanks be to God**', is provided, but it is unclear when these words may be said – during or after the sprinkling.

Reflecting on these two generally welcome forms of Thanksgiving for Holy Baptism, one does wonder whether the symbol is surrounded by too much wordiness (cf. Kavanagh 1993). Nevertheless, the element of water is prominent and is an integral element in the liturgical action. And as with all liturgical action, it is the way in which the element is handled and used in the celebration which is the decisive factor.

Mention must also be made of the use of water for the ceremony of the washing of the feet at the Eucharist on Maundy Thursday, for which provision is made in the *Times and Seasons* volume. (The washing of feet has also appeared as an optional element in the new service for the ordination of deacons as a sign of the humble service, patterned on Christ's servanthood, to which those to be made deacon are about to enter.) The foot-washing after the reading of the Gospel (John 13) on Maundy Thursday is a long-established custom and is traditionally accompanied by the chant *Ubi caritas*: 'Where charity and love are, there is God.' However, it seems as though the origins of this liturgical custom are found not in the Eucharist but in a baptismal context. Ambrose is hard-pressed to explain how the foot-washing (the *pedilavium*) became established as a post-baptismal ceremony after the sacramental bath in Milan. It was unknown in Rome, but was practised elsewhere – in Gaul, in Spain, and possibly in East Syria too. A vestige survives in the eighth-century Irish Stowe Missal, but here the emphasis is placed on how the baptized must follow the example of Christ's service. The account of Jesus washing the feet of the disciples in John 13, though admittedly placed in the context of the Last Supper, can be interpreted as primarily a baptismal pericope, in that it concerns the bond between Christ and the disciple. When Peter objects to having his feet washed by the Lord, Jesus explains that this has to be done to him if he is to have any 'part' or share in his Lord's imminent fate, that is, his suffering and resurrection. Indeed, some scholars have suggested that in some primitive Christian communities the washing of feet might have constituted the ritual act of baptism itself, whereby the person was joined to Christ (see Spinks, *Early and Medieval Rituals*, p. 52). Martin Connell has written: 'Since the church, following Jesus' example, has been washing feet as a sign of humility since the fourth or fifth century, it may strike us as odd that footwashing would have been an initiatory rite. However, it might have been so, not only in Aquileia, but also in the community of John's Gospel before the writing of the Gospel' (Johnson and Phillips 2004: p. 86).

More *Times and Seasons*

Our reliance on God's grace to refresh and restore us can be symbolized through the use of water in our liturgical celebrations and times of prayer together. Water can be used (albeit occasionally) at particular seasons of the Christian year as a form of preparation for the Eucharist as the penitential rite. An example drawn from *New Patterns for Worship* for the season of Advent is provided by Gordon-Taylor and Jones (2005: pp. 36–7). I would add that during the sprinkling of the water it would be appropriate to sing the Advent Prose with its refrain, 'Drop down, you heavens, from above, and let the skies pour down righteousness.' But an even stronger case could be made for the occasional use of such a rite during the season of Lent. After all, in the western tradition it is the season most closely associated with the preparation of candidates for baptism at Easter. In addition, the themes of Lent invite us to reflect on the dry desert of our own wilderness and on our need for the 'gentle dew of God's mercy' which leads us back to the absolving waters of baptism, a sentiment voiced by W. H. Auden:

> In the deserts of the heart
> Let the healing fountain start
> (Auden 1991)

The Roman Missal provides a Rite of Blessing and Sprinkling of Holy Water, the *Asperges*, as an alternative form of preparation to replace the opening penitential rite for the Sunday Mass. After the greeting of the people a vessel containing water is brought before the priest, who says that the water is used to remind us of our baptism. Then one of the three prayers of blessing is said, and the ministers and people are sprinkled while an appropriate song, such as the *Asperges me* with the refrain 'Wash me, and I shall be whiter than snow' (Psalm 51.7), is sung. The rite concludes with a simple prayer of absolution which looks towards the celebration of the Eucharist.

A modified form of the *Asperges* is provided in *Times and Seasons*, as an alternative form of absolution in the penitential rite, directed for use in the Easter season. An occasional rite such as this, like the Thanksgiving for Baptism on the Feast of the Baptism of Christ, could, if practicable, take place at the font. This would provide something of a staged service allowing for movement for the whole congregation. There would need to be sufficient space for the people to gather round the font, and then after the sprinkling, for the whole gathering to process into the nave for the Ministry of the Word, perhaps singing Psalm 42 with its congregational refrain: 'As the running deer seeks the flowing brook, even so my soul longs for you, my God.'

God's blessing and forgiveness and the gifts and graces of the Spirit symbolized in the ritual use of water all ultimately relate to the sacrament of baptism. And what we have discussed in these pages are the liturgical forms which provide ritual opportunities for these divine gifts to be bestowed, renewed and released in the lives of God's people. In classical Anglican terms, those who come to take their place at the Lord's Table Sunday by Sunday are renewed in that baptismal covenant, which binds us each to another and asks of us a commitment to the care of the earth and all its people, especially those who thirst for justice and peace.

3

Oil

SIMON JONES

Historical background

Anointing with oil was common to many ancient cultures. While the ritual use of oil in the Judaeo-Christian tradition may have its origins in the cultic practices of Egypt and Mesopotamia, oil was also used for non-religious purposes. Within the Graeco-Roman world, for example, it had domestic and medicinal uses: it was burnt in lamps, rubbed on wounds and used in cooking. Athletes would rub their bodies with oil before a contest and scented olive oil was rubbed into the skin after bathing.

In the Old Testament, the cleansing properties of oil are recognized in the anointing of lepers during the process of atonement (Leviticus 14.15–20). Oil is also used to anoint objects – the stone at Bethel (Genesis 28.18), for example, and the tent of meeting and its contents: 'you shall consecrate them, so that they may be most holy; whatever touches them will become holy' (Exodus 30.29). And a prophecy of Isaiah refers to a shield being oiled to make it supple and fit for battle (Isaiah 21.5).

More importantly, however, the Hebrew scriptures describe the anointing of priests, kings and, possibly, prophets (Exodus 30.30; 1 Kings 19.15–18; 1 Samuel 16.11–13; 2 Samuel 5.3; 1 Chronicles 16.22). The purpose of these anointings is not medicinal, but to confer a new identity upon an individual by consecrating him for a divine purpose and filling him with grace and power to fulfil it. This is the theological and ritual context within which the anticipated deliverer and redeemer of God's chosen people becomes known as the Anointed One – *Meshiah* (Messiah) in Hebrew and

Christos (Christ) in Greek – a title which Jesus applies to himself when he quotes Isaiah 61.1 in the synagogue at Nazareth: 'The Spirit of the Lord is upon me, because he has anointed me' (Luke 4.18).

There is no biblical evidence to suggest that, during his ministry, Jesus anointed others, although he appears to have commissioned the Twelve to anoint the sick with oil (Mark 6.13) and refers to oil and wine being used to anoint the victim in the parable of the Good Samaritan (Luke 10.34). Recognizing Jesus' true identity, the woman who comes to the house of Simon the Pharisee shows the extent of her love for Jesus by anointing his feet and wiping them with her hair (Luke 7.37–50); and at Bethany the woman's anointing of Jesus' head (Matthew 26.6–13) anticipates the rituals of burial.

As for anointing in the liturgical life of the early Church, the letter of James explicitly refers to elders praying over the sick and 'anointing them with oil in the name of the Lord' (James 5.14). It has also been suggested that references which link anointing to Christians being sealed with the Spirit, such as 2 Corinthians 1.21–22, refer to a physical rather than merely metaphorical anointing with oil within the context of initiation, though this is by no means certain (see also Ephesians 1.13; 4.30; 1 John 2.20, 27).

However such references are interpreted, it is clear that, at least by the third century, anointing with oil played a significant role within the rites of Christian initiation. In succeeding centuries, although the way in which oil was used varied quite considerably both within and between regions, anointings can broadly be characterized as 'exorcistic' or 'therapeutic', particularly in relation to preparation for baptism, 'Christic', marking out the new identity between the baptismal candidate and the Anointed One, and 'pneumatic', expressing the bestowal of the gift of the Spirit in the process of initiation.

Thus, for example, in the East Syrian *Acts of Judas Thomas* (third century), the therapeutic nature of the pre-immersion anointing is expressed as oil is poured upon the head of a candidate about to be baptized: 'Heal her of her old wounds, and wash away from her her sores, and strengthen her weakness' (Syriac version, ch. 121). A Christic understanding of anointing is brought out in one of the hymns of the fourth-century poet Ephrem the Syrian: 'From whatever angle I look at the oil, Christ looks out at me from it' (*Hymns on Virginity* 7.14). Early in the fifth century, Theodore of Mopsuestia links the post-immersion anointing with oil to the descent of the Spirit upon Jesus at his baptism in the Jordan: 'This shows that the Holy Spirit never leaves him, just as the anointing attaches to those who are anointed by men with oil and never leaves them. You, too, then, must be sealed on the forehead' (*Baptismal Homily* 3.27). This pneumatic anointing was often distinguished from all other types by being performed with a perfumed oil known as chrism or, in Greek, *myron*, which was made from olive oil mixed with balsam or spices or another fragrant unguent.

Anointing with oil was equally common in the Church's ministry to the sick and was understood holistically, as a ritual accompaniment to prayer for spiritual as well as physical healing. As such, it was an extension and continuation of the salutary work begun in baptism, encompassing exorcism, repentance and forgiveness of sin as well as restoration to health. These elements are combined in a prayer for the blessing of oil and water found in the fourth-century *Apostolic Constitutions*: 'Now sanctify this water and this oil through your Christ, in the name of him or her that has offered them, and grant them a power to restore health, to drive away diseases, to banish demons, and to disperse all snares through Christ our hope' (*Apostolic Constitutions* 8.29).

Whereas during the first five centuries of the Church's history oil for the sick was usually blessed by a bishop, as in the *Apostolic Constitutions*, it is clear that its administration during this period was not restricted to the clergy. Thus, Christians would often keep blessed oil at home to use as it was needed, either to anoint or to take as medicine. By the ninth century, however, the ritual use of oil had become, along with penance and viaticum, the Church's sacramental ministry at the time of death and, as such, was administered by the clergy. No longer understood within the context of prayer for the healing of body and soul with the expectation of recovery, by the twelfth century this anointing had become the last rite to be received by a dying person before their death, known as 'extreme unction'.

Unlike initiation and healing, the use of oil in connection with ordination is a relatively late development, with no clear evidence as to its use until the eighth century, where the Gallican rite witnesses, first, to the anointing with chrism of the hands of a newly ordained presbyter and, later, of a new bishop also. According to Paul Bradshaw, by giving a literal interpretation to its reference to 'the dew of heavenly unction' in the prayer for the ordination of a bishop, the Roman rite also introduced an anointing with chrism, which was inserted into the middle of the ordination prayer; but this time it was an anointing of the head (Bradshaw 2006: p. 223). Although such a reference may originally have been intended to be understood metaphorically, it is easy to see why it was literalized in later centuries: 'May it [the dew of heavenly unction] flow down, O Lord, richly upon their head; may it run down below the mouth; may it go down to the uttermost parts of the whole body, so that the power of your Spirit may both fill them within and surround them without' (Leonine Sacramentary; Bradshaw 1990: p. 216).

A number of the rites considered thus far have included prayers for the blessing of oil alongside formulas for its administration. Although the *Apostolic Tradition* (early third century), traditionally attributed to Hippolytus, describes the blessing of oils at Easter, immediately before they were used in the rites of Christian initiation, the present-day practice of the episcopal blessing of oils of the sick, of catechumens and of chrism within the context of a Eucharist on Maundy Thursday can be traced back to the Gelasian Sacramentary, compiled in the eighth century. In addition to the use of oil at initiation, ordination and in ministering to the sick and dying, anointing has also had a part to play in rites for the coronation of a monarch, the consecration of churches and altars and the dedication of bells.

At the Reformation, anointing with oil was judged to be a superstitious ceremony by the reforming churches and, as such, was removed from their liturgical rites. In the Church of England, the 1549 Prayer Book retained anointing after baptism and as part of the visitation of the sick, but neither of these found a place in the second Prayer Book of 1552. Indeed, despite various attempts, not least by the nineteenth-century Tractarians, to call for the restoration of anointing in the Church of England, it was not until the publication of *The Alternative Service Book* (*ASB*) in 1980 (for initiation) and *Ministry to the Sick* in 1983 that its optional use was given official authorization.

Anointing within a baptismal context

Of all the revised services which fill the several volumes entitled *Common Worship*, none exerts greater influence over the shape and content of the others than the rite of holy baptism. That this is the case is not simply the result of the sequence of liturgical revision (although *Common Worship: Initiation Services* (*IS*), published in 1998, was the first volume to be issued with the *Common Worship* title). Rather, it is the natural liturgical consequence of a renewed and strengthened theology of initiation which has consciously presented baptism as 'a sacrament of significance in its own right that points Christians to their true identity, character and calling within the body of Christ' (*Common Worship: Christian Initiation* (*CI*), p. 315) rather than an isolated rite of passage. As such, baptism has not only become the liturgical centrepiece around which the other initiation services cluster, such as the catechumenal rites on the way, and the confirmation and reconciliation services, but it has also left its mark on more distant rites, such as healing and wholeness and ordination, whose text and ritual have been shaped and influenced by its distinctive ecclesiology.

This liturgical and theological development, arguably the most significant to have emerged from the *Common Worship* revision, provides the framework for our consideration of anointing in contemporary worship. We have already seen that the use of oil within the rites of Christian initiation is an ancient and enduring feature of many traditions, resonating with and ritualizing rich biblical imagery, and that there has been a close association between the anointing of the sick and of those preparing for baptism. The fact that, within the space of a decade, anointing with oil has achieved a greater degree of authorized visibility than ever before in the history of the Church of England is surely not unrelated to this recovery of the centrality of baptism and its new-found status within the family of *Common Worship* rites.

Common Worship: Christian Initiation, Rites on the Way

Within the volume of initiation services, Rites on the Way provides for a signing with the cross as part of the Welcome of Disciples on the Way of Faith and the Call and Celebration of the Decision to be Baptized or Confirmed or to Affirm Baptismal Faith. In the first, which is intended to 'mark the beginning of the formal journey of faith for new disciples who can answer for themselves', there is no encouragement to use oil. In the second, which follows a period of exploration for those who have experienced regular involvement in the Christian community, the minister asks the candidates whether they will receive the sign of the cross as a mark of Christ's love for them as they explore his Way. Note 3 permits this signing to take the form of an anointing by a priest with pure olive oil, which should be consecrated for this purpose by the bishop. Anticipating the formula for the signing with the cross in baptism, 'Christ claims you for his own. Receive the sign of his cross', the same note directs that if a candidate for baptism is anointed during the Call, oil is not used again before the candidate is baptized. This signing or anointing imitates the ancient rite for the making of a catechumen, and is similar to that found in the Roman Catholic Rite for the Christian Initiation of Adults (RCIA).

A service such as this, which may be used for different categories of candidate with varying spiritual backgrounds, runs the risk of blurring the distinction between them, and this is particularly problematic when it comes to distinguishing candidates for baptism from those to be confirmed or who wish to reaffirm their faith. Although a separate form of words is provided for the signing of those candidates who are already baptized, the notes do not make it clear whether or not this may take the form of an anointing. If, as the note would seem to suggest, the oil of catechumens is used to anoint candidates for baptism, it is surely not appropriate for the same oil to be used for the baptized.

Moreover, if the use of oil *is* reserved solely for candidates for baptism, then the anointing becomes the only visible sign which marks them out from others who are using this rite. If this is the case, then it is important to consider how this anointing is best performed; a point which is reinforced by the fact that none of the spoken texts in this rite make any reference to oil or anointing. The explanation given in the note that such an anointing reflects athletes preparing for a contest is surely unsatisfactory, since very few candidates will be half-naked or prepared to have their whole body covered in oil at this point in the service!

To afford the oil greater visibility, thought needs to be given to how it is stored as well as how it is applied. It may be possible for the oil to be kept in a glass cruet or jug and put on a table in a prominent position throughout the service, rather than being soaked into some cotton wool enclosed in a small silver stock. When it comes to the signing, in full view of the congregation some oil could be poured from the jug into the palm of the minister's hand or a shallow bowl, and taken from there to sign the candidate's forehead. If there are a number of candidates and/or several sponsors are joining in the signing, then pouring a larger amount into a bowl may be more practical. As a general rule, whenever oil is used, it is more important to be concerned about making the anointing a visible and generous symbol than about making a mess.

Christian Initiation: Holy Baptism

In the service of Holy Baptism, Note 10 makes a clear distinction between two sorts of oil, and indicates that one (the oil of catechumens) is more appropriate for the optional anointing before baptism, and the other (the oil of chrism) for the optional anointing after. Once again, the image of an athlete preparing for a contest is used to explain the anointing before baptism at the signing with the cross, whereas the post-baptismal anointing with chrism is described in Christic as well as pneumatic terms, 'expressing the blessings of the messianic era and the richness of the Holy Spirit' (*CI*, p. 100).

Taking each of these anointings in turn, whether or not oil is used the consignation which takes place before baptism comes as a ritual response to the decision made by the candidates. The juxtaposition of cross and oil after the decision symbolizes God's invitation to salvation, the candidates' acceptance of the same once-for-all act of God in Christ, and the Anointed One claiming them as his anointed children by marking them with his sign, the sign from which flows the grace by which the candidates will be strengthened to 'Fight valiantly as a disciple of Christ'. All of this makes perfect theological and liturgical sense, but here again we are confronted by a series of texts which do not mention or even allude to oil or anointing.

By uniting the signing with the cross with an anointing with the oil of catechumens, the Church of England has superimposed two separate and distinct liturgical actions within the process of the catechumenate: the making of catechumens and the anointing of catechumens preparing for baptism. In the modern Roman rite these two ritual acts remain distinct and, in the case of RCIA, are performed on separate occasions. The signing of the forehead (and the senses) without oil happens only once as part of the Rite of Acceptance into the Order of Catechumens, whereas anointing with the oil of catechumens may be celebrated at any time during the catechumenate, as well as on Holy Saturday or immediately before the profession of faith in the baptism rite itself.

As a result of the Church of England's uniting of these two ritual acts, the symbolism of the anointing can easily be obscured by the signing with the cross, not least since the minister cannot rely on the spoken word to highlight or to interpret it. As with

Rites on the Way, if oil is used, careful attention needs to be given to the way it is stored as well as how it is applied.

Much more suggestive, however, is the prayer after baptism, where anointing with the perfumed oil of chrism is permitted. The reference to God pouring upon the candidate the riches of his grace, and the petition for daily renewal by God's anointing Spirit, does give more of a clue as to what might be going on ritually as well as theologically. To anoint with chrism during this prayer is not to say that this is the moment at which the Spirit is conferred. Rather, it is to make use of a vivid sign which identifies the candidate as one who has been reborn, who has become a new creation, who has been filled with the life of the Spirit and, then looking forward, prays that this new identity in Christ might characterize the candidate's life from this day forward. The Liturgical Commission's commentary suggests that, to distinguish this anointing from that at the Decision, the chrism may be applied in the shape of a chi-rho, signifying *Christos*, the Anointed One (*CI*, p. 336). To me, this seems unhelpful and very obscure. More importantly, it does not reflect the language of the prayer, which is not sufficiently Christic to warrant such an image. In this instance, it would be far simpler and much more powerful to reflect Old Testament practice and, using a larger quantity of oil than for a consignation, pour chrism over the crown of the head – thus making a bold and vivid gesture which can be easily seen and smelt.

Christian Initiation: Confirmation and the Affirmation of Baptismal Faith

Common Worship permits anointing with the oil of chrism to accompany confirmation as well as affirmation of baptismal faith. The Liturgical Commission's commentary makes clear that 'the view has been taken that it is consistent with the Western tradition not to limit the use of chrism to confirmation'. It goes on to extrapolate from this that the use of chrism is permitted at affirmation of baptismal faith and reception into the Church of England

(*IS*, p. 348). Curiously, neither the rite of reception nor any of the Notes associated with it make any reference to anointing in this service.

In confirmation and affirmation, although there is no ambiguity as to whether oil may be used, no clear guidance is given as to when this may take place or how it may be administered. My impression is that most bishops anoint at confirmation as they address the candidate, 'God has called you by name and made you his own' and then lay hands on the candidate, as the rubric directs, during the 'Confirm, O Lord' petition. However, if anointing is, as the commentary suggests (*IS*, p. 345), an accompaniment to prayer, it is strange that chrism should be administered as the bishop addresses the candidate, rather than God.

Comparing *Common Worship* once again with the Roman liturgical tradition, in the latter the anointing of the forehead with chrism follows the laying on of hands, and is accompanied by the performative formula 'Be sealed with the gift of the Spirit'. Since such a form of words makes a stronger connection between confirmation and the reception of the pneumatic gift than many Anglicans would find doctrinally acceptable, one option might be to anoint with chrism in silence after the laying on of hands. But, once again, this raises problems of performance and interpretation.

Anointing while addressing the candidate may well be the best solution, not least since it can be seen to affirm the identity of the confirmand as one who has been born again by water and the Spirit in baptism (whether earlier in the service or at any time in the past) and now seeks prayer for the ongoing activity of God's anointing and strengthening Spirit in his or her life. In terms of performance, as with the oil of catechumens, the chrism may be brought to the bishop in a glass jug and poured into a shallow bowl. To anoint with the sign of the cross on the forehead seems the most appropriate ritual gesture.

Further complications arise if anointing is used for those who wish to affirm their baptismal faith. First, if this happens at a service where candidates are also confirmed, since both receive the laying on of hands (and can be anointed) there is a possibility, as with Rites on the Way, that the distinct identities of these two groups can be confused. That aside, the prayer over the candidates, in which the president asks God to 'equip them with the gifts of your Holy Spirit and fill them with faith in Jesus Christ', is followed immediately by the laying on of hands accompanied by a formula which, unlike confirmation, addresses the candidate rather than God: '*N*, may God renew his life within you that you may confess his name this day and for ever'. Since this is the only formula which follows the prayer over the candidates, it probably makes best sense of the rite to anoint with chrism on the forehead with the sign of the cross while the president is saying the candidate's name.

Times and Seasons: Pentecost

Although not one of the initiation services, the Liturgy of the Feast of Pentecost in *Common Worship: Times and Seasons* (*TS*) also provides for anointing, either with chrism or with oil blessed specially for the occasion, as part of an innovative rite of gathering. Here anointing accompanies prayer for personal renewal. Although no formula is provided for this optional anointing, the *berakah* ('Blessed are you . . .') prayer which precedes it (for use when oil is to be blessed) makes clear its purpose: 'Let it be for them a sign of your acceptance and adoption, your equipping and empowering'. For those churches which use chrism for the rites of initiation and where the oils may have been received on Maundy Thursday (see below, p. 54), it will surely be appropriate to use chrism on this occasion as well. If so, the thanksgiving prayer may still be suitable, not least since it follows the *Common Worship* formula which we will encounter elsewhere, asking that God's blessing may 'rest upon those anointed with this oil in your name' rather than on the oil itself. No guidance is given as to how or by whom the oil should be administered. Since, in other rites, anointing is restricted to the clergy, it is probably best to follow that practice here, although lay members of a ministry team could well be involved in the laying on of hands, if that is used as part of the ministry of prayer. As to how the oil should be administered, since God's people are being equipped and empowered for service, it may be appropriate to anoint the palms of the hands with the sign of the cross as well as or instead of the forehead.

Ordination services

Unlike many of the texts we have considered thus far, the formulas for the optional anointing of newly ordained priests and bishops do themselves refer explicitly to the use of oil, setting the call to ordination within a baptismal ecclesiology: 'May God, who anointed the Christ with the Holy Spirit at his baptism, anoint and empower you'. In the ordination of priests, the connection between spoken word, ritual act and the object of the petition is particularly strong, where it is the hands anointed by the bishop which will be used to bless and reconcile. The position of the anointing before the welcome and after the giving of the Bible (if it is not postponed to the dismissal) makes clear that it is a secondary symbolic action which is separate from the ordination prayer.

In terms of performance, the oil of chrism should be used and the anointing will often be administered while the newly ordained kneel before the president. In the ordination of priests, Note 14 directs that it is the palms of the hands which may be anointed; whereas when a bishop is ordained, the equivalent note refers to the anointing of the head. Although practised in some dioceses, the ordinal does not make provision for the anointing of deacons. Historically, the hands of the priest were anointed, since these were to handle holy things in the celebration of the Eucharist; and the head of the bishop was anointed, in the same way that priests and kings were anointed in the Old Testament. In the deacons' rite, an optional foot-washing comes at this point in the service.

As with initiation, it would be appropriate for the oil to be placed somewhere visible to the congregation, or at least to the ordinands, throughout the service. In the ordination of priests, it may be possible to pour the oil into the new priest's hands. If this is done, the candidate could stand side-on to the congregation with hands held out, palms upwards, over a bowl, while the bishop pours the oil over them. If a large quantity of oil is used, it is important not to wash it off immediately afterwards. It should suffice for a towel to be provided to dry the hands. When a bishop is ordained, the archbishop will normally anoint the forehead with chrism, making the sign of the cross.

Wholeness and healing

Pastorally, the rites associated with wholeness and healing are more sensitive than any of the services we have considered so far, and are set within a carefully considered theological framework in the introduction to *Common Worship: Pastoral Services* (*PS*). The link between baptism and healing has already been discussed, and this connection is emphasized at the beginning of the introduction, setting prayer for healing (and the use of oil within it) within a baptismal ecclesiology. The introduction begins: 'Baptism witnesses to God's gift of salvation, in which he gathers people into the new creation in Jesus Christ. Baptism points to the way in which God in Jesus Christ is overthrowing an order of life corrupted by sin and death and bringing to birth a renewed creation, a creation alive with the healing presence of God's Spirit' (*PS*, p. 9).

Within the various rites of wholeness and healing, a form is provided for the laying on of hands and anointing as part of a diocesan or deanery occasion; within the context of the Eucharist for occasional use or as part of the regular liturgical life of a parish; and, of course, as part of ministry to the sick and the dying (the latter appears at the beginning of the material for funeral services).

One interesting point of comparison between the first two of these services relates to the prayer over the oil. Both are *berakah*-style prayers, similar to that already encountered in the Pentecost liturgy, and although the prayer in the diocesan or deanery rite is longer than that for parish use, they both contain identical petitions with regard to what is being blessed: 'By the power of your

Spirit may your blessing rest on those who are anointed with this oil in your name'. However, the notes reveal that only the longer form is considered to be a prayer of blessing, whereas the shorter is intended for occasions when oil has previously been blessed. According to Note 5, the use of the former is justified 'not only to ensure an adequate supply of oil' but also 'to provide a prayer of thanksgiving at the heart of the rite' (*PS*, p. 25). Although a couple of paragraphs shorter, the second prayer functions in exactly the same way, but for some reason is considered inadequate to bless. A further interesting feature about this provision is the short form of prayer over the oil provided in the supplementary texts, which does petition God to bless the oil in order to bring healing to the anointed: 'Sanctify this oil, that those who are anointed with it may be freed from suffering and distress, find inward peace, and know the joy of your salvation' (*PS*, p. 47).

The point which the note makes about the importance of having a prayer of thanksgiving at the heart of the rite is an important one. One of the problems with the ritual use of oil, when compared with symbols such as bread, wine, water or fire, is that it is rarely used in conjunction with a prayer of thanksgiving. With the possible exception of the Liturgy of Pentecost, this has been true of all the rites we have seen so far. A eucharistic prayer, prayer over the water, or *Exultet* not only functions as a prayer of blessing, but also provides the theological and liturgical framework within which the symbol operates and gains its power within the story of salvation, whether it says 'Who, in the same night that he was betrayed, took bread', or 'Over water the Holy Spirit moved in the beginning of creation', or 'In love you led your people with a cloud by day and with a pillar of fire by night'. The prayers of thanksgiving associated with the three oils are found in the Chrism Eucharist, which we shall consider shortly, but only in these two rites of wholeness and healing does such a thanksgiving preface the anointing. The reason for this, of course, is that in initiation and ordination anointing is very much a secondary and optional symbol, and each of these rites already contains thanksgiving prayers which relate to other primary ritual actions.

In the services of wholeness and healing, the formula for anointing gives verbal articulation to the ritual action. In whatever context the anointing is being administered, at home or in hospital, at a large diocesan occasion or a monthly parish 'healing Eucharist', the formula is the same: 'I anoint you in the name of God who gives you life. Receive Christ's forgiveness, his healing and his love'.

The notes which relate to ministry to the sick refer to Canon B37, which requires that the priest should use 'pure oil consecrated by the bishop of the diocese or otherwise by the priest himself' and that the anointing should be made on the forehead with the sign of the cross. That said, Note 4 also permits anointing of the hands (*PS*, p. 73).

The way in which the oil of the sick is administered will depend very much on the individual context. In a home or at a hospital bedside it is most convenient for the oil to be soaked into cotton wool and carried in a stock or other suitable container. Whether it is appropriate to anoint the palms of the hands as well as the head will depend partly on the condition of the person who is sick and, as with the administration of communion, in a hospital setting it is often wise to ask medical staff for guidance.

When the anointing of the sick takes place within an act of public worship, the same general principles apply as for initiation and ordination. If possible, the oil should be visible and poured into a shallow bowl before being administered.

Anointing also has an important part to play within ministry to the dying. In the *Common Worship* provision anointing with oil is not the 'last rite', but administered between the laying on of hands and Holy Communion. The notes refer again to Canon B37 and to anointing by a priest using oil blessed for the purpose (*PS*, p. 235). Here, obviously, there is no *berakah* prayer of thanksgiving but, as in the Coronation rite, the short formula for anointing is followed by a lengthier prayer which unpacks the significance of this ritual act and also links it to the inward unction of the Spirit: 'As you are outwardly anointed with this holy oil, so may our heavenly Father grant you the inward anointing of the Holy

Spirit.' As with anointing of the sick, the priest is encouraged to anoint the forehead and, if desired, the hands, but the manner of the anointing will once again depend on individual circumstances.

Times and Seasons: Chrism Eucharist

Although the *ASB* printed a collect and appropriate readings for the blessing of oils, *Common Worship* goes much further by providing an historical note as well as a number of resources for a chrism Eucharist. If the Church of England is to recover confidence in the ritual use of oil, then particular thought needs to be given to the way in which the Chrism Eucharist is celebrated and, not least, who is encouraged to attend it. In many dioceses, whether it takes place on Maundy Thursday or on another day in Holy Week, it is advertised as a rite for the clergy. One reason for this is that the Chrism Eucharist is also the occasion for the renewal of ordination vows. Although, as we have seen, the Canons state that anointing with oil can only be performed by bishops and priests (though deacons may anoint at Holy Baptism), the oils are not the property of the clergy, but are God's gift to the whole Church, to be used in rites of initiation, ordination and healing.

If, as has been suggested, wherever possible oil should be poured rather than being administered with the thumb, it will be necessary to make sure that generous quantities are blessed. Those who have responsibility for preparing the oils also need to make sure that enough balsam or perfume is added to the oil of chrism so that it is sufficiently fragrant to be distinguished from the other two, as it can be used more effectively if it can be smelt as well as seen. In the western tradition, deacons have traditionally carried the three oils to the bishop to be blessed. Note 4 refers to these three deacons being vested in distinctive colours: purple for the oil of the sick, green for the oil of baptism, and white for the oil of chrism. At the Chrism Eucharist the appropriate dress for the deacons of the oils would be alb, stole and dalmatic.

Common Worship gives no indication as to when the oils should be blessed. Historically, in the western tradition, the blessing of the oil of the sick took place before the end of the eucharistic prayer, and the blessing of the other two oils after communion. In the modern Roman Rite, it is permitted for the entire rite of blessing to be celebrated after the Liturgy of the Word. The Church of England has tended to follow this practice, and it is most common for all three oils to be blessed between the Peace and the eucharistic prayer. A hymn or anthem is often sung as the deacons carry the three oils to the bishop. *Common Worship* provides for each deacon to announce the name of his or her oil as it is presented. For the blessing, the oil may be held in front of the bishop or placed on a suitable table. Each prayer over the oil is in the style of a *berakah*, in which God's blessing is asked to rest on those who are anointed, rather than on the oil. It is appropriate for the bishop to extend his hands to the *orans* position (open and uplifted) as he sings or says each prayer and to bring them together again as the people respond. If desired, the bishop himself can pour the balsam or perfume into the oil of chrism and mix it with a spoon before it is blessed. The prayer over the chrism is traditionally concelebrated, expressing the way in which priests share in the sacramental ministry of their bishop. To follow this custom, it may be appropriate for all priests (and any other bishops present) to extend their right hands towards the chrism as the bishop says the prayer over it. At the end of the Eucharist, the oils should be carried by the deacons to wherever they are going to be distributed. To honour the consecrated oils, incense may be carried at the head of this procession (if it has been used at the Eucharist) with the deacons walking behind the candles and cross.

Times and Seasons: the Reception of Holy Oils

Since it is likely that only a relatively small group within any Christian community will be able to attend a daytime chrism Eucharist, *Common Worship* also provides a rite for the reception of oils at the beginning of the Liturgy of the Last Supper on Maundy Thursday (*TS*, p. 292). Although optional, its use is to be strongly recommended, since it provides a wonderful opportunity to raise the profile of the oils and to make the important link between the rite celebrated by the bishop and the ongoing sacramental ministry of the parish in which the oils will play a significant part. The rubrics suggest that the oils may be carried in the entrance procession. If possible, they should be carried in glass jugs or cruets so that they can be easily seen. It may be appropriate for a hospital visitor or someone who has recently been absent from the worshipping assembly through illness to carry the oil of the sick; a candidate for baptism or a godparent to carry the oil of catechumens; and an ordinand or someone involved in preparing people for confirmation to carry the oil of chrism. The oils are presented in turn and, after each, the president says a short prayer which makes useful reference to the way in which it will be used. The oils should then be taken to the place where they are reserved.

Conclusion

In July 1982 a form for the blessing of oils was rejected by the General Synod, with one member describing the Liturgical Commission's proposals as 'rather like a form of white magic' (General Synod 1982: p. 349). Twenty-five years later the liturgical landscape looks very different, and it is hard to believe that anointing has attained such broad coverage in the rites of *Common Worship*.

There is nothing magical about the ritual use of oil in Christian worship; nor is it simply a visual aid. Rather, anointing with oil, in whatever context it occurs, is a sacramental action which, through the power of the Spirit, effects an encounter between the Anointed One and the anointed. There is a depth to this symbolic action that the Church of England is only beginning to discover. By paying careful and creative attention to the way in which oil is used, the Lord's anointed may be helped to discover their true identity as those called to 'fill the world with the sweet fragrance of Christ's gospel and be built up as living stones into a temple filled with the Holy Spirit' (*TS*, p. 292).

4

Light

CHRISTOPHER IRVINE

Most of us now find ourselves living not only in over-lit build-ings, but also in an over-lit urban environment, and, together with the increasingly 24/7 social life in our city centres, any real differ-ence between day and night is a long-forgotten experience. And in all probability, few of us have experienced complete darkness. Our urban nightlife is lived under the diffused glow of sodium street lighting and the glare of security lights, and yet, paradoxi-cally, the night can still be experienced as a threatening time, a time when we do not feel as safe as we might during the hours of daylight.

In these conditions we might ask how far the primal experi-ence of the natural rhythm of day and night, light and darkness, informs our consciousness, let alone the pattern of our own lives. On the other hand, how do we reckon with the phenomena of lighting candles and tea lights when anonymous crowds of people gather in public spaces to remember a tragic event, or of torches carried in night-time political demonstrations and candles lit dur-ing an anti-war vigil? Whatever we make of this, the lighting of candles still touches the popular imagination, and it would seem as though the placing and carrying of lights, whether on a protest march or as an act of remembrance, is an acting-out of a deeply felt and often unarticulated desire for the coming of a time when circumstances will be different from how they are presently ex-perienced. Perhaps the most dramatic event of this kind was the so-called 'Candlelight Revolution' of 15 March 1989, when some 75,000 people bearing candles filled the streets of Budapest to protest against Communist rule. When people light candles at a political rally on the occasion of a national crisis, they may be expressing a residual human need to indicate a significant time, and to make some gesture towards a hoped-for future.

Even so, our public symbolic behaviour, as we witnessed during the time of the death and funeral of Diana, Princess of Wales, is an interlude in the way we usually operate in the world. Our social worlds, if not atomistic, are private, and the assumption underlying our public behaviour is that we all live in a world which in principle is capable of rational explanation. The seventeenth-century priest-poet John Donne had presaged the dominance of such a scientific, as opposed to a symbolic, worldview when he wrote:

> And new philosophy calls all in doubt,
> The element of fire is quite put out . . .
> ('An Anatomy of the World')

And yet Donne's contemporary, the French writer and mystic Blaise Pascal, struggling to express his experience of God, latched on to the image of fire: 'FIRE. The God of Abraham, of Isaac, and of Jacob, not the God of philosophers and scholars'. The metaphorical use of fire for the experience of a divine encounter recalls the story of how YHWH revealed his presence to Moses in the burning bush (Exodus 3.1–6), an image, incidentally, appropriated by the writer of the prayer for the blessing of the Easter candle, known as the *Deus mundi conditor*, in the eighth-century Gelasian Sacramentary. The living flame of a candle is drawn from the primal element of fire, that dangerous, unpredictable and consuming element of light and heat, which is the symbol of our encounter with the living God in Christ. Playing with fire is dangerous, and perhaps in the history of religious practice a number of rites and ceremonies have evolved as a way of controlling this destructive element. The temple in Jerusalem had a perpetually burning lamp, and it seems that some ancient Jewish religious rites involved the carrying of torches and lights (see Psalm 89.15). Pagans greeted the light of the evening lamps, and Christians too came to mark their holy places with lamps, and to place light on their altars to reflect the splendour of their liturgical celebrations. As we shall see, Christians came to bless the source of light, and lit their evening lamps to reveal the living Christ.

The kindling of lights at daily prayer and on Sundays

The use of light in acts of worship serves more than one purpose, and the first is undoubtedly the utilitarian use of lamps and candles to give light at night. An early description of the Christian assembly is set at night-time, and tells how they gathered in a domestic setting for the breaking of bread and that Paul preached until midnight. As the story develops, the incidental detail is given that there were 'many lights in the room' (Acts 20.8). The earliest evidence is slight and sketchy, but other sources confirm this impression that when the first Christians gathered together, they kindled lights. In his letter to the emperor Trajan, Pliny, the Roman Governor in Bithynia in Asia Minor, reported how Christians gathered before daybreak on a 'set day' (presumably a Sunday) to sing a hymn to Christ, as to a god, and then gathered together in the evening for a shared meal together. Tertullian, writing from North Africa around AD 200, tells how the lighting of lamps concluded the Christian common meal (the *Agape*), and a later fragmentary piece of evidence (*Apostolic Tradition* 29) witnesses to a ritual act of the bringing in of a lamp by a deacon as a prelude to the singing of psalms and hymns before sharing the common meal. Pagan sources recount how the appearing of the light of the first evening lamp was met with a greeting, and we might recall the Jewish custom of the lighting of a candle at the beginning of the domestic Sabbath meal. But the Christian practice undoubtedly has other and perhaps more influential antecedents, and, as illustrated by the vocabulary of the light prayer in *Apostolic Tradition* 29, the focus was not on the element of light in itself, but on the figure of Christ.

By the fourth century in Cappadocia, the kindling of a lamp had long established itself as an introductory rite to daily evening prayer. In his treatise *On The Holy Spirit*, Basil the Great alludes to the established custom of greeting the light not in silence, but with a hymn of thanksgiving, and another source tells how his brother, Gregory of Nyssa, heard the alluring sound of the hymn to greet the light as he sat at the bedside of his dying sister Macrina (*On the Holy Spirit* 29).

In a recent study of the history and theology of daily prayer, Gregory Woolfenden (2004) argues that the early Church followed the Jewish custom of reckoning a 'day' from sunset to sunset, and that the natural movement from night to day provided the template for celebrating daily Christian prayer. Christians tended to gather for prayer together in the evening and morning, and in doing so made remembrance of the Paschal mystery of Christ through the natural movement from night to daylight. This coordination of the natural rhythm of night and day, of movement from darkness into the light of the day with Christ's resurrection, was explicitly made by some very early Christian writers. Clement of Rome, for example, said: 'Day and night show us the resurrection; night sets, day rises; day departs, night comes.' A similar symbolic frame of reference is reflected in what the later Church Orders say about the pattern of daily prayer. A striking example is the *Testamentum Domini*, variously dated between the second and fourth centuries, which intriguingly speaks of the evening, when the sun sets and the natural daylight dies, as eliciting our praise and causing us to 'show an image [*eikon*] of the Resurrection' (2.24), which presumably refers to the living flames of the evening lamps. Tertullian corrected the apparent misunderstanding that Christians were sun worshippers by indicating that the appearing of morning light at dawn was a symbol of Christ's risen presence. Writing from Alexandria, his contemporary Origen underlined the symbolic significance of praying towards the east, suggesting in his treatise on prayer that praying towards the east, where the sun rises, symbolized the soul beholding the rising of Christ, the true light (*De oratione* 32). This orientation for prayer had a direct influence on the design and layout of churches, and demonstrated their eschatological consciousness, their being alert to the promised coming of the risen Christ in glory, for 'as the lightning comes from the east and flashes as far as the west, so will be the coming of the Son of Man' (Matthew 24.27).

As forms of daily prayer developed in differing locations and cultural contexts, the ceremony of the lighting or bringing in of a lamp, accompanied by praise and thanksgiving, became a key feature and came to be called the Lucernarium. In the Christian assembly, or even at home in the case of the aged and infirm, the first kindled evening light was greeted with a prayer of praise and thanksgiving, which in a church setting developed, as we have seen, into a song of praise, the most ancient of which is the *Phos hilaron*, 'O gladdening light, O grace'. The content of this hymn is strikingly similar to the deacon's prayer of praise offered at the bringing in of the lamp at the Christian shared meal, and again focuses on the figure of Christ, who has 'shone upon us and revealed an inextinguishable light'. Here the light of the lamp not only has a utilitarian function in providing necessary light at dusk, but is also symbolic. The *Testamentum Domini* includes in its list of directions regarding the ordering of a church the simple directive: 'Let all places be lighted for a type and for the readings' (1.19). The provision of lights is obviously for the practical purpose of reading, but also as a 'type', a term which we might translate as 'figure' or 'symbol'. It is Christ who brings light into the darkness of the night. The act of kindling the light is a ritual gesture symbolizing the coming of Christ to humanity to enlighten us and to blaze the way to the Father through his own death and resurrection.

Following earlier Anglican revisions (notably those of the ECUSA *Book of Common Prayer* in 1979, and the Church of Canada's *The Book of Alternative Services*, 1985) and the provision in *Celebrating Common Prayer*, an optional form for the Blessing of the Light, consisting of a greeting, a prayer of thanksgiving, and a hymn or canticle, is provided in *Common Worship: Daily Prayer* as an alternative to the set Preparation at the beginning of Evening Prayer. The prayer of thanksgiving asks that even during the dark hours of the night we might remain 'children of the day', that is, children of the resurrection. The Blessing of the Light can be observed on weekdays as well as on a Sunday, and adds an element of ritual and movement to what might otherwise be a fairly static and verbal liturgical celebration centred around the Word. The candle to be lit needs to be of a suitable size, ideally a standard candle placed before a lectern set in the middle of the choir. This provides a key visual focus and links the element of light with the scripture readings, reinforcing the sense of God's Word being 'a light to my path' (Psalm 119.105). After the candle is lit, presumably with a taper, the prayer of thanksgiving may be offered by the officiant standing before the lectern. If a hymn is to follow, other candles, such as the altar-table candles, may be lit from the central lucernarium candle during the singing of the hymn. Even if the provisions of *Daily Prayer* are not used, an occasional Lucernarium can effectively precede a Book of Common Prayer (BCP) service of Evening Prayer, especially during the season of Advent, with its rich imagery of light and darkness, and during the season of Easter. When the BCP is used, the Office can begin with the opening versicles and responses after the lighting of the candles.

In *Daily Prayer* the sense of the rhythm of Morning and Evening Prayer as being a remembering of Christ's death and resurrection finds a voice in the similarly optional material to begin Morning Prayer which is called 'The Acclamation of Christ at the Dawn of the Day'. This Acclamation may replace the Preparation at Morning Prayer, on any occasion, we are directed, and is effectively a greeting of the resurrection, the dawning of the Sun of Righteousness.

A further directional note in one of the optional forms of penitence which may be used with Morning Prayer in the *Common Worship* daily prayer provision (*DP*, pp. 91–7), suggests the lighting of a candle, presumably as a visual focus, before the invitation to those gathered to recall and then confess their sins. This might strike some as a fairly arbitrary use of liturgical symbolism, redolent of that school of liturgical thought which says 'candles with everything', but this innovative ritual act accompanying the prayer of penance does resonate with a strand of Johannine writing in the New Testament which presents the dawning, saving judgement of Christ as the coming of light into the darkness of our sin: 'And this is the judgement, that the light has come into the world, and people loved darkness rather than light because their deeds were evil. For all who do evil hate the light and do not come to the light, so that their deeds may not be exposed' (John 3.19–21; cf. 1 John 1.7–9; 2.8–11; 1 Corinthians 4.5).

Common Worship: Times and Seasons

The image of light recurs, albeit in different registers, through the round of the Christian year. The Christian calendar is generally taken to be cyclical, but as it has developed, what we can trace are in fact two epicycles. The one that has come to be taken as the first runs from Advent to the Feast of the Presentation (Candlemas), and the second runs from the beginning of Lent to the Feast of Pentecost. Each cycle has its designated preparatory period, and the two complexes of feasts, Pasch/Easter and Christmas/Epiphany, are respectively festivals of light. The first is the coming of the light of judgement and the revealing of the incarnate Christ as the light of the world in the Christmas cycle, and the second is the light of the risen Christ and the kindling of the divine love in human hearts in the Easter cycle. Our use of lights in these two seasons of the Christian year is a way in which we symbolize the theological truths rehearsed in the unfolding Christian story in the turning of liturgical time. The ritual kindling and carrying of lights in our services during the seasons of Christmas and Easter is an enactment of that liturgical play in which we may come to apprehend the truth of both the coming and the resurrection of Christ. In other words, our ritual actions allow the meaning of what we celebrate to get to us, to be inscribed 'deeply into the bone' (Grimes 2000) so that we are able to 'do the truth' (1 John) and to live what we celebrate through the Christian year.

In terms of the historical development of the Christian year, the Easter cycle, undoubtedly the more primitive, takes precedence. Its light is the saving *work* of the incarnate Christ in his death and resurrection, while the Advent/Christmas cycle casts the light back from Christ's saving work to his *person*, or who he is. Recent studies have shown how the Christmas cycle slowly evolved in response to the various fourth- and early fifth-century controversies which sought to find an adequate language with which to speak of Christ's humanity and divinity. The final doctrinal formulation in the Nicene–Constantinopolitan Creed resorts to philosophically charged and symbolic language, denoting Christ, the eternal Son of the Father, as the 'Light of Light'. The fixing of Christ's birth in the Christian calendar on 25 December in the West (calculated from the date of the Passover) asserted the cosmic significance of Christ against the Roman political *imperium*, as that was the same day as the festival of the birth of the unconquered sun (*natalis solis invicta*), established by the emperor Aurelian *c.*270. It also reinforced the theological polemic against heterodox views of the nature and person of Christ, with its rhetoric of light dispelling the blindness of ignorance (see Roll 1995: p. 221).

At that time the hymns sung daily at morning and evening were richly metaphorical and applied the imagery of light to Christ as the 'morning star' heralding the dawn (cf. 2 Peter 1.19; Revelation 2.28), and the 'sun of righteousness' (promised in Malachi 4.2) which 'shall arise, with healing in its wings'. These and similar images of light found their way into the liturgical texts and rituals as Epiphany, Christmas and Advent gradually took form in the western Church and became universally fixed in liturgical calendars by the second half of the fifth century, albeit with some geographical variations, such as the actual duration of Advent.

The season of Advent prepares us for the coming, or arrival (*adventus*), of Christ. The Evangelist John appropriated the theme of light from the Jewish Feast of Tabernacles, and designated Christ as the light of the world who comes to enlighten all people

(John 8.12; 1.9). Christ is the promised light and glory of God (Baruch 5.5–9), but the Advent message is a warning as well as a promise, for the light that Christ brings is the searching light of God's judgement. Both Paul and John exhort their readers to live their lives in the light of Christ's love (Romans 13.12; 1 John 2.8–10), to bring Christ's love to light in their attitudes and actions and thereby prove themselves to be 'children of the day'.

Thus the dominant metaphor and symbolic register for Advent is again darkness and light. The coming of Christ is the coming of light. Zechariah, the father of John the Baptist, in words familiar to us as the *Benedictus*, the morning Gospel canticle in *Daily Prayer*, foretold the dawning of the Messianic age in terms of the imagery of light: 'the dawn from on high will break upon us, to give light to those who sit in darkness and in the shadow of death, to guide our feet into the way of peace' (Luke 1.78–79). Scriptural passages with the double theme of darkness and light, such as Isaiah 9.2–7, 'The people who walked in darkness have seen a great light', read at the Midnight Mass on Christmas Eve, provide the dominant scriptural context for this seasonal cycle of liturgical readings. In the high latitudes of the Northern Hemisphere the nights in the winter season are very long, and the Roman festival of the birth of the unconquered sun undoubtedly provided some relief in the gloom. But the image of Christ as light, although resonating with the Roman cult of the sun as well as with some earlier Egyptian forms of belief, was, as we have seen, largely fired by the primitive Christian eschatological hope for the full realization of God's purposes, encapsulated in the prophecy of Malachi 4.2 quoted above, a text which Christians soon applied to the coming of Christ (see Talley 1986: part 2). The appearing of that light for eastern Christians is celebrated on the Feast of the Epiphany (6 January), which focuses not so much on the birth of the Christ-child, but on the baptism as the supreme showing of Christ as God's beloved Son. The epiphany episodes in John's Gospel are seen as pointing to and effectively anticipating the glory of Christ's death and resurrection, that 'hour' of his glory according to John's scheme of things. The liturgical season of

Epiphany has appropriated the Egyptian focus on Christ's baptism, with which Mark's Gospel begins, the Matthean story of the Magi, and the Johannine sign of the turning of water into wine at Cana in order to reveal the radiance of Christ's appearing in time, the guarantee of his second coming in glory, that total inrush of transforming divine luminosity.

In our celebrations, the building up of Advent light can be dramatically shown by using an Advent wreath, and placing it prominently in church as a symbolic visual focus. The Advent wreath, originating in seventeenth-century Germany and popular in Nordic countries, is a largely pedagogical means of ritualizing the mounting expectation as the candles are lit on the successive four Sundays in Advent, in turn representing 'the patriarchs', 'the prophets', 'John the Baptist' and 'Mary', and finally a large central candle of Christ is lit on Christmas Day, or more generally, at a crib or carol service on Christmas Eve. Three sets of prayers for each Sunday are provided in *Common Worship: Times and Seasons*. It is an ideal opportunity to involve the children in church, and although it works well as part of a gathering rite, or immediately before the eucharistic Prayer, *Times and Seasons* suggests that the candle may be lit after the Gospel, presumably as a ritual action to complement the Word, and it makes further provision for linking the lighting of the Advent candles with the penitential rite, presumably envisaging the actual lighting of the candle with a taper after the absolution. Particular circumstances in each church will determine how and at which point in the service the Advent candle may be lit. The four candles are traditionally red or purple, with the addition of a central white candle for Christmas, and decorated with evergreen holly and ivy. Whether this Christmas candle has the same symbolic resonance as the Easter candle is a moot point, as it represents what is taken to be an event (the birth of Jesus), and is, therefore, more *commemorative*, rather than *presentational* in the sense of making present the One who is the Alpha and the Omega and Lord of all time.

Nevertheless, if church attendance is an index of what actually speaks to people, Christmas continues to draw large congregations. The social and cultural factors behind the phenomenon of Christmas church attendance, such as its being a counterweight to the indulgent materialism of the holiday season, its sentimental association with children, and the appeal of 'light' in the dark winter solstice in the Northern Hemisphere, are really beyond the scope of this essay. But suffice it to say that these Advent and Christmas customs of kindling lights are an index of an apparently felt need to ritualize our deepest hopes and aspirations. Here indeed we might see the human being as a 'maker of signs', seeking to make the invisible visible through the use of sensible forms and symbolic gestures. The symbol of light, neutral in itself, works in relation to darkness, and in staging our worship, equal consideration should be given to how we might move – sometimes literally, as in a candle-lit procession – from darkness to gradually increasing illumination. An evening Christmas carol or crib service can begin in semi-darkness with the electric light being dimmed or reduced after the congregation has taken its place. This will be especially effective at the lighting of the candle proposed in *Times and Seasons* outlines for a Christingle and a crib service.

As a natural symbol, light shows the way ahead, and the Christmas light, intensified by the glimpses of divine glory in the weeks of Epiphany (which in one part of the ancient Christian world, Cappodocia, attracted to itself the very name 'Feast of Lights'), leads us towards a crucial turning point, a feast in which the light, paradoxically, enables us to face the darkness. The feast of Candlemas, falling on 2 February, has had a varied history, combining a variety of themes, and has been variously named as aspects of this day have assumed prominence. It has been a feast of Mary, the Purification, and the now-preferred Presentation, commemorating both the offering of the infant Christ in the Temple, and the meeting of Christ and the elderly Simeon and Anna. Processions of one kind or another have long been associated with this festival, as has the carrying of lights, hence its German name *Lichtmesse*, which literally means 'Light-mass'. The prayers in the old liturgical books of the West have focused on the element of light, and have generally been prayers asking for protection and recognizing our need for purification in order that we might receive the benefits of Christ's sacrifice.

Common Worship: Times and Seasons provides three options for the procession of lights: at the beginning of the service, after the reading of the Gospel, or at the end. As the Gospel speaks of the bringing of Christ into the Temple at Jerusalem, an entrance procession (perhaps mirroring the Palm Sunday procession with its twin themes of sacrifice and entry into the holy place) suggests itself as the most appropriate arrangement, ideally setting off from an adjacent building, or moving from a side chapel into the main space of the church where the liturgy will be celebrated. When the people have gathered with their candles, the scene is set, prayer is offered, and appropriate hymns and anthems are sung as the procession makes its way into and around the church. The individual candles used in the procession could be relit for the Gospel, a passage in which Simeon welcomes the light and glory of God in Christ. This song of Simeon, familiar to us as the canticle *Nunc dimittis*, with its opening words: 'Lord, now you let your servant go in peace', makes an apt alternative to the Dismissal and could be sung at the end of the service. If it is sung here after the post-communion prayer, the ministers and servers could then leave in silence, thereby shifting the mood, and pointing us towards the coming season of Lent, and that greater Holy Week silence of Good Friday, when a 'sword pierced Mary's heart' and Jesus was led to the cross 'as a sheep dumb before its shearer' and darkness came to cover the earth. This returns us to the very *source* of light for the Christian, the Paschal mystery of Christ's death and resurrection.

It is generally, though not universally, agreed that the lighting of the Easter candle on Holy Saturday, symbolizing Christ being raised from the dark caverns of death, developed from the lighting of the evening lamps at dusk during evening prayer. In addition, the fourth-century pilgrim Egeria recorded what seems to have been a weekly practice on a Saturday evening in Jerusalem, of bringing a light from the Sepulchre in the Anastasis church (where a lamp perpetually burnt) from which the individual tapers of those gathered for such a popular devotion would be lit. In this way the light spread to create what Egeria described as 'a blaze of light'. Pilgrims returning home would have told their tales and so liturgical practices spread and were adapted to more local circumstances, especially in the celebration of the Easter Vigil. Night services, of course, required some illumination, but the appearing of light at the Easter Vigil soon came to represent the appearing of the risen Christ. At the celebration of the Easter Vigil in Spain, for instance, a light was secretly kindled in a sacristy and then brought into a dark church, where the people would welcome the new light with the triple acclamation 'Lumen Christi' (the light of Christ). The history of the gradual adoption of a special Easter candle, or candles, lit at the Easter Vigil, with all its fascinating regional and contextual variations, is told by A. J. Macgregor (1992). The practice of lighting an Easter candle is now common and transcends church traditions.

Common Worship: Times and Seasons, Festivals, provides three patterns for the celebration of the Easter Vigil on Holy Saturday. The first begins with the Service of Light, the second with the Vigil readings, and the third is an outline for a more informal Easter dawn service, which might well be celebrated outside, on a hilltop, or at the beach. For each service, the congregation gathers in the darkness of the night, and in the second pattern (B), what is envisaged is reminiscent of the gathering of people around a fire to hear the stories which remind them of their identity and speak of what has shaped their corporate identity as the people of God. Some light is required for the readings, and the introductory notes in *Times and Seasons* say that the Vigil in the second pattern should begin with the lighting of a small fire or light for the extended reading of the stories of salvation, and categorically warns that this light must not be confused with the Easter light kindled after the extended series of Old Testament readings. Such an arrangement certainly resonates with our understanding of Vigil services, but presents challenges of both a practical and symbolic character for those planning and leading the Easter

Vigil. A more satisfying arrangement is provided in the first pattern (A), where the Vigil readings are preceded with the kindling and praise of the Easter candle, for at this celebration the readings are to be read (and heard) in the light of the Risen Christ (see Irvine 1996: p. 7).

Times and Seasons urges us to consider our use of the church building, and mention is also made in more than one place of the use of the building and use of a bonfire for the Easter Vigil. The lighting of bonfires to mark particular times and events certainly chimes with folk memory, and the lighting of a bonfire at the beginning of an informal dawn service in an outside location certainly has a popular appeal. The lighting of Easter candles from a 'new fire' became fairly common practice in northern Europe during the eleventh century, and in this case might well represent a Christianization of the earlier pagan practice of lighting bonfires to hasten the spring and the season of new growth. The making of bonfires for Holy Saturday was certainly encouraged by a directive in the 1970 *Missale Romanum* that a 'large fire' should be prepared. The primal element of fire has a place in the celebration of such a hidden mystery of the resurrection, and possibly resonates with mythology, evoking the phoenix who rises from the ashes. But in the context of the Easter Vigil as it has developed in the West, the primary purpose of the new fire is to provide a flame from which the Easter candle is lit, and not to be a spectacle in itself. Apart from the absurdity of a minister attempting to light a candle from a furiously burning fire, there is also the fact that the Easter candle, as the primary liturgical symbol of the celebration, should not be dwarfed by a huge fire. A small brazier is quite adequate for the occasion, and should be positioned just in front of the main entrance of the church, with the congregation informally gathered around it. Once the candle is lit, it should lead the procession into the darkened church, with the congregation following behind with their individual candles. At each of the three stations, with the acclamation 'The Light of Christ', the light can gradually be passed around the congregation.

In being carried at the head of the procession into the darkened church the burning Easter candle becomes the 'pillar of fire' which led God's people of old from slavery to freedom, oppression to joy, and which also symbolizes Christ himself. What makes this night so different from other nights is that our liturgical time connects us to that saving time when Christ entered the darkest corners of death so as to lead humankind into the light of a new day, the dawn of God's new creation, as is shown in the Byzantine Icon of the Resurrection, the Anastasis.

The candleholder for the Easter candle should be placed immediately in front or by the side of the *legilium* or reading desk from which the readings will be declaimed. Impressively large, fixed candle-stands for the Easter candle were common in twelfth-century Rome. At San Clemente, for instance, one is integral to the structure of a pulpit designed for the singing of the *Exultet*. A magnificently carved stone Paschal candleholder, 5.6 metres in height, is to be seen in San Paolo fuori le Mura. Around the base of this candle-stand is an inscription which reads: 'As the tree bears fruit, so do I bring light and gifts, and announce joy'. The overall decorative scheme of carving presents the Easter candle as a symbol of the whole Christ, crucified, risen and Lord of the Church.

In our celebration of the Service of Light, once the minister (traditionally a deacon, if there is one) has placed the candle in its stand, and the people are in their places, the candle is blessed by the singing of the *Exultet*, or Easter Praise (traditionally sung by a deacon), which forms the climax of the Service of Light component. The individual candles held by members of the congregation should be blown out after the singing of the *Exultet*, and relit for the baptismal component of the Easter liturgy, thereby drawing the connection between the Paschal mystery and the meaning of baptism. This connection is made most explicit if the Easter candle is plunged into the water during that part of the Prayer of Thanksgiving Over the Water where God is asked to bless it. (For an account of the intriguing historical precedents for this practice, see Spinks, *Early and Medieval Rituals*, pp. 132f.).

Pastoral need, such as a multi-church benefice, may require the use of more than one Easter candle. When the author was an incumbent of a two-church benefice, two candles were lit at the Vigil, carried together into the darkened church, and then placed on either side of the *legilium* for the Vigil readings. The resource provision in *Times and Seasons* includes, in the form of an Appendix (App. D), a form for the 'Welcoming of the Paschal Candle' to be used in a building where the Easter Vigil has not been celebrated. Weather permitting, the congregation could assemble outside before the main entrance of the church and then be joined by the minister and an assistant bearing the Easter candle. The Easter candle should then be greeted and individual candles for the congregation lit during the singing of a suitable refrain, such as the Taizé chant 'The Lord is my light, my life and my salvation'. When all the candles are lit, the minister carrying the Easter candle leads the whole assembly into the church for the remaining service, symbolically claiming that architectural space as belonging to God's kingdom of light.

It is customary to keep the Easter candle alight throughout the Easter season, the great 50 days which reaches its culmination with the Feast of Pentecost. *Common Worship: Times and Seasons* provides a special 'Blessing of Light' to be used on the Feast of Pentecost which neatly shifts the symbolic register from the light of the resurrection to the fire of God's love, the fire of the Holy Spirit distributed to empower each of us for Christian love and service. After this festive Lucernarium prayer, designed to follow from a post-communion prayer as an extended rite of dismissal, individual candles held by the congregation are lit from the flame from the Easter candle, and a set piece of prose leads into a statement concerning the mission of the church in the locality. There are then a series of questions and congregational responses, which alas are focused rather exclusively on the life of the congregation, with scant reference to the engagement of the church in the wider community. A rubric directs that if there are no further services in the building, the Easter candle is to be extinguished in silence before the recessional hymn.

Illumination and baptism as enlightenment

The ancient description of baptism as 'enlightenment' was noted in Chapter 2, but we might develop further this aspect of the dramatic rite of baptism as illumination, symbolized in the giving of light. The old adage was that Christians are made and not born, and today that sense of becoming Christian is highlighted by the central metaphor of journey. And so, the *Common Worship* Initiation Services are complemented by a whole raft of 'Rites on the Way', providing signposts to mark out our Christian pilgrimage as those called to live in the light of Christ (Ephesians 5.8–9). As the baptized are called by the One who came to enlighten everyone (John 1.9), it is appropriate that a further ceremony, the giving of a lighted candle, should follow the actual water-washing of baptism. In the rich imagery of the Psalter, the Lord is our light (27.1) who enlightens us (18.29; 36.9), and leads us in his light (43.3; 89.15). Further, a conjunction of the two baptismal symbols of water and light is found in Psalm 36: 'with you is the fountain of life; in your light we see light' (v. 9). Those (predominantly adults) who were being prepared for baptism in fourth-century Jerusalem were referred to as the *Photozomenoi*, literally those who were being enlightened, and in the instructions of Cyril of Jerusalem he alludes to an unexplained ceremony, apparently taking place on the first day of Lent, when the candidates carried torches in procession. At this point Christian initiation was celebrated in the evening, and a fourth-century document associated with the church in the city of Milan, *De lapsu virginus*, describes the 'shining light of the neophytes' as the newly baptized and anointed candidates returned from the baptistery to gather before the altar for the celebration of the Eucharist. Celebrating initiation during the hours of the night, of course, invited a play on the themes of darkness and light, but what we have here in *De lapsu virginus* is not a metaphorical reference (as in Denys the Areopagite's designation of newly baptized being 'clothed in light') but an actual candlelit procession. However, no indication is given as to exactly what was said or done, or at which precise point the newly baptized were given a lighted candle or torch for this procession. An allusion to a torchlit procession of neophytes is also made in an Easter sermon delivered by Pope Gregory the Great in sixth-century Rome, and although no reference is made to when the torches were lit in the rite, the symbolic significance of the light is spelt out in terms of the lamps borne by those who go out to meet the heavenly bridegroom (see Matthew 25.1–13).

By the tenth century in Rome the custom of giving the newly baptized a lighted candle after the water-bath was well established. But what did this actually symbolize? In terms of the historic practice and our reading of the texts of the rites, we can see that the baptismal light had been variously presented as the light of the risen Christ and the light of Christ's first and second coming. The earliest textual evidence points to the prominence of the latter (Dendy 1959: p. 127). Certainly in England, up to the eve of the Reformation, the words accompanying the giving of the light in the Sarum baptismal rite again evoked the scene of the Advent parable of the young women awaiting the arrival of their master through the long and dark hours of the night (Matthew 25.1–13). A rubric in the Sarum rite directed that a burning candle was to be placed in the hand of the newly baptized infant, as it is called by its name: 'N, . . . receive a lamp burning and without fault: guard your baptism, keep the commandments, so that when the Lord comes to the wedding you may meet him together with the saints in the heavenly hall'. Here the symbolic action is associated with the theme of purity as well as with the hope of the newly baptized being welcomed into the heavenly banquet with all the saints in light.

Thomas Cranmer removed the giving of a light to the newly baptized, presumably regarding it as a 'dumb ceremony', from the service of baptism in the first English Prayer Book of 1549, and it was not restored until the revisions of the late twentieth century, and then only as an optional post-baptismal ceremony. In the family of Anglican rites, it first appeared as an optional ceremony in the ECUSA rite for Holy Baptism in its 1979 *Book of Common Prayer*, although no words were given to accompany this post-baptismal ceremony. The ECUSA *Book of Common Prayer* defines Christian baptism as baptism in water *and* the Spirit, and the desire of its compilers to heighten the pneumatic or Spirit aspect of baptism probably made them anxious not to introduce a ritual element which would detract from the movement from water-bath to anointing. Thus the giving of a light to the newly baptized is a silent and optional ceremony. But it is not without symbolic reference. It is suggested in one of the notes that the baptismal candle may be lit from the Paschal candle. This direction is made explicit in the revised Roman Catholic rites, with the intention of signalling a direct link between baptism and the Paschal mystery of Christ's death and resurrection. Such a symbolic reference is reinforced by the custom, outside the Easter season, of placing the Easter candle alongside, or in close proximity to, the baptismal font.

The option of giving a lighted candle to the newly baptized (or more likely to a parent or godparent) immediately following the baptismal water-washing was adopted in the Church of England's *Alternative Service Book* (*ASB*, 1980), and occurs in the same position in *A New Zealand Prayer Book* (1989), which suggests that the newly baptized may be given a lighted candle by a representative of the congregation. Although the *ASB* rubric directing the giving of a candle made no specific reference to the Paschal candle, again a note indicates that it may be lit from the Paschal candle. The giving of the candle was accompanied with words, drawing on the New Testament imagery of the baptized being called 'out of darkness into [God's] marvellous light' (1 Peter 2.9; cf. Ephesians 5.8) and of how the Christian's manner of life should bring God's mercy and kindness to light (Matthew 5.14, 16; cf. Philippians 2.15). This New Testament imagery was taken by commentators on the service of baptism in the *Alternative Service Book* to point to the mission of the baptized people of God in and for the world. The baptized are called to be 'lights in the world', not by drawing attention to themselves but to show a way of life that is both lived towards God and which mirrors his transforming glory in a social world darkened and brutalized by human sin and violence.

This focus on mission, a much overworked term in contemporary Christian rhetoric, led the compilers of the baptismal rite in *Common Worship* to place the ceremony of the giving of the candle to the newly baptized at the dismissal, the 'sending out' at the conclusion of the service. It occurs as part of an optional dismissal, 'Going Out as God's People', in Rite Two of Baptism in the more recent Church of Ireland's *Book of Common Prayer* (2004). In *A Prayer Book for Australia* (1995), a simple versicle (drawn from the words of 1 Peter 2.9) accompanies the handing over of the light, eliciting the congregational response adopted from the *ASB*: 'Shine as a light in the world to the glory of God the Father'. *Common Worship* retains this response, but precedes it with words drawn from Colossians 1.13–14: 'God has delivered us from the dominion of darkness and given us a place with the saints in light', and heightens the element of *missio*, of the baptized being sent out, with the dismissal: 'Go in the *light* and peace of Christ'.

The Pastoral Introduction included in *Common Worship: Initiation Services* states rather weakly that the baptismal light is a 'picture of the light of Christ'. But what is permitted in the rubrics and reinforced in the Notes shows a greater appreciation of the power of this multivalent symbol of light. An interesting feature in the *Common Worship* provision is the suggestion that a large candle (a specific preference for the use of the Easter candle is expressed in the Notes) is lit in that earlier part of the baptismal service known as the Decision. The Liturgical Commission's commentary suggests that the ritual act of lighting a candle at this stage is to act as a symbolic counterpart to the renunciation of darkness in the Decision. In some ancient rites, in Jerusalem and in Syria for instance, when the candidates renounced sin and evil, they literally faced west, which symbolized the realm of darkness, and then turned towards the east, the realm of light, as they made their allegiance to Christ prior to entering the bath of regeneration. The forms of service provided for the Corporate Renewal of Baptismal Vows, in both *Initiation Services* and *New Patterns for Worship*, replicate the rubric that allows for the lighting of a large candle.

This brief historical survey reveals the wide evocative range and associations of the light given at baptism. Which particular meanings are evoked will depend exactly how and in what part of the service the giving of the candle occurs. The close association of the giving of the candle with the dismissal undoubtedly has an evident ritual coherence, but this does not preclude the use of the Easter candle in the rite. Indeed, the Easter candle can be used to heighten the sense of baptism as a transitional journey, from death to life and from darkness to light. It is particularly effective if it is carried to lead the ministers and baptismal party in procession from the chancel step, where the parents and god-parents may be gathered for the Decision, to the font (if it is in its traditional location near the entrance to the church building), and then back into the nave, where the candle might be placed either in close proximity to the altar-table, if the baptism is taking place in the context of the Eucharist, or in front, or by the side of the *legilium*, if the baptism takes place in the context of a Service of the Word. Either way, the use of the symbol and physical movement will enhance the ritual action, and will provide a central and unifying symbol for the whole celebration. After the Blessing, the candidates, parents, godparents and sponsors, carrying their lit candles, could form a recessional procession led by the servers and ministers through the nave to the back of the church, where they could be informally greeted by members of the congregation as they leave the church building.

Finally, in baptism we are, of course, joined to the whole Body of Christ and come to share in the communion of saints, of those who were 'lights in their several generations'. From earliest times it was customary to place lights to mark the burial site of Christian martyrs and saints. Indeed, the custom of having burning lamps and candles within a church building, especially around the altar, finds its origin in part in this primitive custom. Lights mark the holy place, and increasingly today provision is made to light a candle before an image or painted icon of a saint. Even in places where there are no such statues of Mary or of some other saint, provision is made for worshippers and visitors to light a 'prayer candle'. Prayer, especially for another person, is one of the many languages of love, and as the wax of the candle slowly consumes itself as it burns, so the lighting of a candle as a prayer can be a symbolic gesture of self-giving love. It can burn for someone in need, or for a departed loved one, and its flame can evoke that deepest Christian hope for the remaking and healing of God's creation, when all will be transfigured by the divine glory: 'And the city has no need of sun or moon to shine upon it, for the glory of God is its light, and its lamp is the Lamb. By its light shall the nations walk' (Revelation 21.22–24a).

5

Incense

BENJAMIN GORDON-TAYLOR

In the Anglican tradition positive assessment of, and theological reflection on, the use of incense has often been diverted by concerns about legality and related desires to establish how much use, if any, can be demonstrated in the centuries between the Reformation and the Tractarian liturgical revival. However, while it was perhaps ironic that the main scholarly work on the subject should have been written by an Anglican, Atchley's massive 400-page study (1909) is thankfully no exercise in polemic, and remains unsurpassed in detail. Even so, in the Church of England incense has at times played an unhelpful role as a symbol or focus of ecclesiastical dispute, and this persists to some degree at the local level, where it can still be perceived with suspicion as an indication of clerical desires to make an unwilling parish 'high church'. Nevertheless, the positive symbolic value of incense has been rediscovered by many communities who would perhaps at one time have felt it to be inappropriate: cathedrals are a good example. This has happened to such an extent that incense cannot really any longer be seen as the indicator of one ecclesial tradition. Accordingly, some indication is needed of what the history of its use in Christian liturgy reveals about the theology and symbolism of such use, and some guidance is required as to its practical use as a symbol in the rites of *Common Worship* specifically.

History and symbol

Incense is a feature of the history of religions, Christianity among them. As such, it had symbolic significance and practical use long before the emergence of the Church. Atchley presents extensive evidence for this. In the ancient cultures of India, Egypt, Greece and Rome the properties of incense found a place in secular and religious contexts as a means of underlining celebration or the solemnity of an occasion, as a means of giving honour (thus symbolic of status), as a vehicle of exorcism, and as sacrifice to gods. Some of these associations recur in the Christian Middle Ages, but most obviously and significantly for Christianity it is the many references to incense in the Hebrew scriptures which provide more immediate background. There are many instances of incense used practically or figuratively in the Old Testament. These vary in their context, which is sometimes ambiguous and by no means always approving. While these Old Testament uses of incense must be seen as part of the background, they do not necessarily indicate a clear progression to later Christian inheritance historically or conceptually, nor should they be seen of themselves as automatically giving legitimacy to Christian use of incense. Most important are the associations in respect of God and the worship of God, and the manner in which incense speaks symbolically of these on account of its natural properties, the effects of its burning and its visual characteristics. As might be expected the religious use of incense features especially in Exodus, Leviticus and Numbers as expressive of sacrificial offering, and in Psalm 141 it appears as directly symbolic of prayer on account of its rising smoke. This becomes the principal Christian symbolic understanding of burning incense. Thus in Revelation 5.8 and 8.3–4 incense is representative of 'the prayers of the saints'. In 5.8 it 'is' these prayers, while in 8.3–4 it is 'offered with' them, its smoke rising 'with the prayers of the saints . . . before God from the hand of the angel'. Origen confirms this sense in the *Contra Celsum*, bringing together Psalm 141 and Revelation to refute Celsus, who 'does not perceive that we regard the spirit of every good man as an altar from which arises an incense which is truly and spiritually sweet-smelling, namely, the prayers ascending from a pure conscience' (8.17). John Chrysostom was more explicit in associating incense with the penitence of the worshippers, again in connection with Psalm 141 (*Commentary on the Psalms* (= 140)).

In the early Christian centuries, however, incense as a potential liturgical symbol was largely viewed with suspicion by Christian apologists, partly from a desire to emphasize the break with Jewish religion and its sacrifices, and probably also on account of its association with the pagan religion of late antiquity in Greece and Rome, where incense had come to play a significant cultic role, for example in the worship of Aphrodite. Tertullian is therefore notably cool in his attitude towards the burning of incense, explicitly *dissociating* it from *any* connection with prayer (*Apologeticum* 30), although accepting its perfuming properties in a non-cultic sense (*De Corona Militis* 10). This reluctance is an aspect of the wider theological and philosophical debate in the first four centuries AD which accompanied, challenged and facilitated the rooting of Christianity. In a sense the negative view of incense is a practical counterpart to the general reluctance among Christian writers to use mystery language in connection with worship in the same period for fear of confusion between Christianity and mystery religions. In both cases, the end of the debate was the occasion for the beginning of a reversal of this reluctance and the discovery of a positive and authentically Christian symbolic value for incense and the linguistic possibilities of mystery language. This no doubt paved the way for the medieval adoption, however unconsciously, of symbolic meanings more reminiscent of pre-Christian cultic use of incense in the classical world – honour and exorcism – while retaining and developing the patristic, penitential and oblatory association.

The specifically liturgical use of incense is not easy to trace historically – there is no early systematic treatment, only incidental references which admittedly may indicate its acceptance as non-controversial after the fourth century. Thus the earliest established Christian use of incense may be as relatively late as the year 311, at the funeral procession of St Peter of Alexandria, and it is later mentioned in Egeria's account of her visit to Jerusalem. Indeed funerals may have originally been the only occasions on which Christians burned incense, and even then more for sweetening the air than for any specifically symbolic purpose. It needs to be remembered that much use of incense from earliest times up to the modern period was openly and intentionally for entirely utilitarian purposes, principally for reasons of fumigation and health, and not exclusively in a religious setting. Where it was used in churches, the utilitarian and the religious purposes could co-exist, as Alain Corbin, writing of eighteenth-century France, graphically notes:

> Fumigation with incense and storax in churches was seen as an act of worship, but it also tended to cause the stench from the corpses underground to be forgotten; experts saw it as a powerful means of disinfection and an effective protection against the putridity of the assembled worshippers.

(Corbin 1996: p. 65)

Although the disinfecting properties of incense were later scientifically shown to be non-existent, in the pre-modern era it is difficult in truth to separate the utilitarian from the symbolic. This ambiguity of incense need not be problematic, since such ambiguity is surely also present in 'the work of human hands', in the eucharistic elements which in the context of liturgical prayer become the body and blood of Christ: they are utilitarian in that they are food for physical sustenance, but symbolic, and indeed more than merely symbolic, in the reality of the sacrificed and risen Christ, in whose self-offering the worshipper participates. The ambiguity of incense mirrors this, except that it engages the sense of smell rather than taste. Indeed, as is commonly stated, the use of incense at the Eucharist ensures that all the human senses are involved in the worship offered, a consideration particularly appropriate in a sensory age, since it gives initial access to the symbolic language of the rite even for those relatively unfamiliar with formal liturgy and its texts: *accessibility* rather than *intelligibility*, at least for the moment. It is possible to participate with one's senses without necessarily knowing the full *meaning* of what is happening and, indeed, to know the meaning but fail to participate on a deep level because symbols have been explained out of existence, their evocation replaced by over-simplified verbal resolution.

In the medieval West incense came to be used liturgically and ceremonially most particularly at the Eucharist, where its symbolic value was principally that of prayer, which can be said to include the dimensions of penitence, association with the eucharistic offering, and the giving of honour to Christ in the sacrament, this last a kind of wordless, visible *Gloria* or eucharistic acclamation. Incense also featured in processions as a mark of honour, sometimes in honour of saints' relics carried therein, and at the procession of the Blessed Sacrament to the altar of repose on Maundy Thursday and on the feast of Corpus Christi. After the Reformation in England incense is believed to have been used in church, almost always burning in a stationary censer (itself the historical precursor of the portable thurible suspended from chains), and sometimes with at least implied liturgical significance, although the fumigatory properties were doubtless also part of the picture. Lancelot Andrewes composed a form of blessing for church plate (to be used in Worcester Cathedral, and incorporating Psalm 141.2 in the formula) that included such a censer (Andrewes 1935: p. 548). He used in his private chapel 'a triquetral censer, wherein the clerk putteth frankincense at the reading of the first lesson' (Staley 1902–3: p. 180). John Evelyn's diary reveals that the Office at the Whitehall Chapel was preceded by the burning of 'perfume' (Harford *et al.* 1912: p. 406), and it is alleged that at Ely Cathedral in the eighteenth century incense was burnt on great festivals (Staley 1902–3: pp. 183–4). George Herbert also enjoined the country parson to burn it at festivals in order to perfume the building, apparently a sort of olfactory decoration along with the strewing of boughs also directed (*The Country Parson*, ch. 13). All of these relatively fleeting mentions point to at least an implicit association with liturgical prayer, and apparently not in the context of the Eucharist. It may be that while they appear to be the exception, their scarcity in fact indicates the normality of the practice – perhaps it was not remarkable enough to merit much comment. Even so, evidence of the purchase of frankincense in the later sixteenth century is often in such a form as to make clear that it was bought for its sweet smell: at St Oswald's in Durham, for instance, it was bought in the 1630s for such use at the bishop's visitation (Staley 1902–3: p. 179).

Catherine Pickstock in *After Writing* sees the physical properties of the visibly burning incense used in the pre-1962 Latin Mass as an interwoven metaphor with multiple layers of suggestion and (although she does not use the word) evocation, in which pilgrimage, penitence and transformation feature highly in a web of allusion:

> To the requests of purgation [the opening penitential rite] succeeds the blessing of incense, which, before we can offer it to God as smoke, must descend upon us as a heavenly cloud, echoing all the Biblical instances of transfiguration. But just as purification cannot be undertaken once and for all, and becomes, like the journey, an infinitely receding task, also, incense is forever destined to vanish . . . [T]hrough the gift of the Spirit, invoked by the incense we *put on* Christ's own purity.
>
> (Pickstock 1998: p. 188)

Seen in this way, the liturgical use of incense is seen as an integral part of the eucharistic liturgy rather than as an optional extra. I would not wish to claim such necessity for incense in the rites of the Church of England, but there is much here of value in support of its use, with the critical and essential implication that it can never acquire an independence of function, but is always subject to, enveloped in and expressive of the contours of liturgical prayer offered to the Father through the Son in the power of the Spirit.

Yet the symbolism of incense is not confined to the *visible* effects of its liturgical burning, as the post-Reformation Anglican examples given above seem to suggest. The symbolic significance of smell itself has been remarked upon by Sperber among others on account of its capacity to *evoke*. In so doing a wider property of symbols is indicated: Sperber compares symbols to smells, in that they evoke, not refer, because the sense of smell is the least rationalized of the senses and provokes gut reactions and not considered intellectual responses. Evocation is not synonymous with meaning: a smell is not easily recalled, but if smelled again it is able to provoke memories and recall associations (Sperber 1975: pp. 117, 118, 148), Thus the symbol remains undissolved by crudely attributed meaning, but in *evoking* draws in the one who encounters it and opens to them the associative and transformative landscape of which it is a part.

There was a strand of olfactory evocation in the medieval cult of the saints, and particularly in the discovery and disinterring of previously lost or hitherto insufficiently honoured remains of a saint, where a sweet smell, evocative of sanctity (literally 'the odour of sanctity'), was by extension one of the indications that the remains were genuine. This became part of the typical structure of medieval hagiography, whose purpose was often not merely to recount the life of the saint but also to lend credibility to their contemporary cult by means of accounts of such discoveries and enshrinings and associated miracles. Smell as a mark of perceived authenticity as well as of holiness was therefore an important part of the evocative symbolic canvas of medieval religion. However, the smell of incense has not entirely lost this sense of authentication and evocation. The smell of the inside of a church building where incense has been used is immediately evocative of the purpose of the building as a place of prayer – a 'serious house on serious earth', as Philip Larkin puts it in his poem 'Church Going' – and evocative of the liturgy that has been and will be celebrated in it. In this it is effectively authenticating and causing to be recognized the building and its function, and further reassuring and authenticating insofar as it indicates, in Eliot's famous words, a place 'where prayer has been valid' ('Little Gidding'). For Sperber, 'each new evocation brings about a different reconstruction of old representations, weaves new links among them, integrates into the field of symbolism new information brought to it by daily life: the same rituals are enacted, but with new actors' (Sperber 1975: p. 145).

Thus the visible and the olfactory properties of burning incense coalesce in the symbolism of prayer, and it is this which remains the principal justification for the use of incense liturgically. Even so, incense as a mark of honour is also associated with the censing of Gospel, altar, sacrament, priest and people. Formerly hierarchical as far as persons were concerned, it is now perhaps best understood in a more general sense rooted in a baptismal ecclesiology, and the renewed sense of the common offering of the liturgical assembly as the priestly people of God. In the terms established by the Vatican II document on the liturgy, *Sacrosanctum Concilium*, influential far beyond the Roman Catholic Church, it acknowledges the Christ present in people, ministers, word and sacrament.

Practice

There have been many works with mandatory or guiding force in their communities, usually as part of ceremonial manuals of wider scope. Therefore the classics of the genre such as Fortescue and O'Connell's *Ceremonies of the Roman Rite Described* (1948) and the Anglican *Ritual Notes* (1947, 1956) include much on the use of incense that is meticulous, detailed and precise. It is accorded high ceremonial importance, as suggested by the inclusion of an illustration, showing how an altar is to be censed, among the front matter of many altar editions of the *Missale Romanum*, a practice imitated by the *English Missal*. Anglican directions sometimes reflect the controversial dimensions of the use of incense, as in Percy Dearmer's *The Parson's Handbook*, which takes great pains to prove legality before any practical suggestions are made (Dearmer 1932: pp. 29–31). More recently Anglican guides have tended to follow the lead of successive editions of the Roman *General Instruction on the Roman Missal*, given the structural and textual similarity of the revised eucharistic liturgies of both communions. These hold good for the rites of *Common Worship* for those who wish to follow them.

The Eucharist

There are several opportunities and possibilities for the use of incense in conjunction with *Common Worship* liturgy: at the Sunday Eucharist, at festivals, at particular seasons and solemn times of the liturgical year. Some brief principles are given in Alcuin Liturgy Guides 3, *Celebrating the Eucharist*, in respect of the Sunday Eucharist using Order One, and these bear repeating:

> Its employment at the entrance of the ministers, the proclam-
> ation of the Gospel, the preparation of the altar and the Eucharis-
> tic Prayer needs to be such as will enhance the offering of prayer
> and thanksgiving and highlight particular moments of divine
> encounter within the celebration of the Eucharist. It is not and
> never has been an accompaniment with any sense of consecratory
> or validating force, and a Eucharist at which it is used, though it
> may be called 'High' or 'Solemn', is no more or no less a Eucharist
> than the simplest of mid-week celebrations. Rather, incense is an
> ancient symbol of prayer, the sweet-smelling savour enveloping
> the assembly as well as the sanctuary as if to communicate the
> commonality of what is being done by all. Consequently there is
> nothing to be measured either by amount of smoke generated or
> elaboration of ceremonial: visible and reverent are more appropriate
> concerns.
>
> (Gordon-Taylor and Jones 2005: 22)

Further directions are given in *Common Worship* at appropriate moments in the detailed description of the rite as one set of
possibilities in that context, and assume the use of incense at the
traditional points of the entrance procession and reverencing of
the altar, the proclamation of the Gospel, the preparation of the
gifts, and during the Eucharistic Prayer. All have prayer, honour
or both as their symbolic intention. Some parishes have tried to
combine the ceremonial of older rites with the *Common Worship*
provision, including the use of incense. This can work, but like
concelebration at an east-facing altar it can also seem anachron-
istically odd, its inherent complexity ill at ease with the relative

simplicity of the revised rites of both Rome and Canterbury, to the extent that the use of incense already mentioned takes on a greater visual importance than is warranted by the totality of the symbolic structure of the rite. Simplicity of ceremonial need not mean dilution of theological content or symbolic power – both can in fact be enhanced, sometimes because ceremonial actions have become *more* visible and more simply and starkly expansive in their performance. If incense is to be used, it ought to be used in such a way as paradoxically to point away from itself, like a liturgical John the Baptist, in order that the mystery of God is glimpsed through it and beyond it with the eyes of the heart and of the soul, as through an animated ritual icon. Both the transparency and the upward movement of the smoke suggest this. In practical terms this will mean a simplification of the associated ritual actions so that these do not become the focus. A worshipping community should also, ideally, be confident enough to say that there are occasions when the use of incense might *not* be appropriate, in order to experience the symbolic value of its absence alongside its still-evocative properties: an emphatic starkness which demands of physical and spiritual vision a different quality of engagement. An occasion for this might well be Ash Wednesday, as if to emphasize the need for clarity of vision in seeking out and confessing the purposes of the heart. Where liturgical symbols are involved, there is a place for the confident exercise of the imagination in harmony with the riches of the tradition.

Common Worship: Daily Prayer

In a bowl or thurible on a stand, placed either before the altar or in the midst of the assembly, recalling the earliest Christian uses and later Anglican ones, incense may appropriately be used at the daily office, particularly when said in common, as is increasingly the practice in many parish churches. In the evening, it may be burnt as a visual expression of Psalm 141: 'Let my prayer rise before you as incense', which forms part of the option of the Blessing of the Light before the office in *Common Worship: Daily Prayer* (pp. 110–11); and the practice is encouraged in the general introduction to that volume (p. xiv). Incense may also be burned (or more grains added) at the Gospel canticle, *Benedictus* or *Magnificat*, in honour of the Gospel and in expression of the prayer offered through these particular texts. The established custom of using incense at solemn celebrations of Mattins or (more usually) Evensong on Sundays and festivals may also feature: here the altar is censed at the Gospel canticle, and incense may be used in a procession.

Another possibility is the use of the bowl of incense as part of a period of intercession: individuals might place grains of incense on the burning charcoal as a mark of prayer for another person or of the thanksgivings and concerns of those present or of the Church more generally.

Holy Week and Easter

Incense may be used honorifically in the 'royal' procession of palms on Palm Sunday, and in the procession to the altar of repose on Maundy Thursday. It is never used on Good Friday. At the Easter Liturgy, the Paschal candle is customarily marked with incense grains in the form of nails (*Times and Seasons*, pp. 408–9), symbolic of the five wounds of Christ and alluding to his sacrifice; the candle may then be censed in honour of the Christ whose resurrection is proclaimed in light and song, and in word at the Gospel of the Eucharist of Easter. The charcoal for the thurible at the Easter Liturgy can be lit from the new fire. Where there is a procession at Evensong, incense may be carried and the altar censed at the *Magnificat*.

Christmas

At the Midnight Mass or another Christmas service, the crib may be censed at its blessing, perhaps using the form in *Times and Seasons* (p. 102); one of the suggested prayers at the crib mentions the three Epiphany gifts, frankincense among them. Incense may also be carried in procession and used at the customary places in the Eucharist.

Epiphany

Frankincense is of course part of the story of the visit of the Magi, and in some places, including the Chapel Royal, is presented as part of the 'traditional offerings' with gold and myrrh. Provision is made in *Times and Seasons* (p. 163) for incense as an option within the Eucharist on the Feast of the Epiphany, and appropriate texts of the 'Blessed are you . . .' form are given for each gift. It might also be appropriate to use actual frankincense in the thurible. *Times and Seasons* also provides material for an Epiphany procession (pp. 184–93; see Notes, p. 185) to take place on the Feast of the Baptism of Christ, including the themes of the Epiphany, the miracle at the wedding at Cana, and the baptism itself. The gifts may be presented as part of this liturgy, and incense used in procession or in a stationary censer: the rite includes an acclamation as the gifts are presented which incorporates the words of Psalm 141 noted above.

The Presentation of Christ (Candlemas)

Incense may be used to accompany the blessing of candles and those who carry them – ideally everyone present. This censing should be done by the president, not the thurifer, and may be preceded by sprinkling. Incense may then be carried in the procession and used at the Eucharist (perhaps omitting the censing of the altar when the sanctuary is reached). At evening prayer, it may be thought more appropriate to cense the altar at the *Nunc dimittis*, as is done in some places, although the particular association of that text with the Presentation does not automatically suggest it – indeed the Song of Mary is all the more poignant on this feast (sometimes seen as, and previously referred to as, a Marian feast also), and so the traditional censing at the *Magnificat* might just as well be retained.

Use of the thurible

The thurible (from *thus*, 'incense') is a censer with a lid suspended on (usually) three chains, with a central chain to raise and lower the lid. It is important that those who act as thurifer acquire a confidence with its use, since it is easy to burn oneself or another person, or inadvertently to allow hot ashes to fall out and burn carpets, altar cloths or vestments. Once lit, the lid and bowl should be assumed to be hot to the touch. The unburned incense is carried in a 'boat', traditionally the shape of a boat, but equally possibly simply a small bowl. A spoon is used to charge the thurible with incense.

The ceremonial use of the thurible is traditionally referred to in terms of 'swings', single or double. In procession the thurible is swung back and forth in line with the direction of walking, at the full length of the chains, taking care not to hit those in front or behind. A 360-degree swing should only be attempted by a skilled thurifer, and only then when in an appropriate space – a lengthy procession in a cathedral might be a suitable occasion, but in truth nothing is added to the symbolism by attempting this, and any heightened drama may well be of the unsought variety if a mistake is made. When censing people or things, the chains are grasped a short distance above the *closed* lid with one hand, the other holding them just below the disc to which their top ends are fixed. The thurible is then held up at approximately chest level and swung towards the person. It is a moot point whether the thurible should be allowed to make audible contact with the chains as it swings – in some places silence is customary. It is also customary in some churches to cense the sanctuary and the assembly with long swings using the full length of the chains – again, this is a matter of local custom. The number of swings is traditionally a mark of the rank of the person or thing being censed – three for the president, two for the deacon, one for everyone else – but as suggested above and in Alcuin Liturgy Guide 3, elaborate censing of hierarchies and persons individually is no longer necessary (Gordon-Taylor and Jones 2005: p. 64).

It may be thought appropriate for the deacon (if present) instead of the thurifer to cense the people as well as the president. At a celebration where the congregation are on three sides or completely surrounding the altar, or even quite easily in other settings, the president may incorporate the censing of the people in the censing of the gifts on the altar, to emphasize the offering of souls and bodies in the corporate eucharistic action. At the censing of the gifts, the cruciform and circular swings pictured in older missals may be replaced with simple swings to centre, right and left. During the eucharistic prayer, the thurible may be swung from side to side, and three double swings towards the elevations if done, and certainly at the greater doxology at the end of the eucharistic prayer. The thurible may be taken out and hung on its stand after the Lord's Prayer (for more on these details see Gordon-Taylor and Jones 2005: ch. 6).

The blessing of incense

It became customary for a form of words to accompany the blessing of the incense by the celebrant at the Eucharist – in translation, 'may you be blessed by him in whose honour you are to be burned' – or similar, but it is as common today for the sign of the cross in blessing to be made in silence. It is not necessary for the president to add and bless additional grains after initially doing so before the entrance procession: instead the thurifer can add more as part of the 'off-stage' preparation of the thurible for the various parts of the rite.

6

Weddings and funerals

SARAH FARRIMOND

'We are all on a journey through life.' So begins *Common Worship: Pastoral Services*. Human beings are born, they pass through puberty, they become adults, many of them reproduce and they grow old or very ill and die. That this is not only a brutal but also an inadequate account of human life is the fundamental reason for pastoral rites. All societies understand human life as something more than this. Parallel to the physical processes of life and death are a whole series of social states. People are infants, then children, then adolescents, then adults. They take on roles in society, they marry and become parents, they retire. Such social states are more various than the physical ones, both within and between different social groups. They impose an order on life, which derives from physical realities, but imputes meaning to them. Social states organize physical exigencies into a story with a clear direction, not only in terms of ultimate destination, but as regards the meaning and significance of the journey.

Rites of passage

The movement from one social state to another is, in most cultural contexts, an occasion for ritual, for prescribed sequences of purposeful actions and words. Ritual in the context of a change of social status is nowadays often, perhaps usually, called 'rites of passage'. This concept was identified by the anthropologist Arnold van Gennep in a book of the same title in 1908, drawing on his own and other people's primary research. That research

93

consists of a cross-cultural analysis of rites by means of which individuals pass from one socially defined state of life to another. He argued that such rites, evident in all societies, have three clear stages: 'separation', in which a person leaves their old status; 'liminality', where the initiate exists between two states of life, in a kind of chaotic social limbo; and 'incorporation', in which the person re-enters society with a new status (van Gennep 1960 [1908]: p. 21). These stages may well be spread over a considerable period of time and will involve, in many cases, numerous different ritual acts. The rituals associated with each of these transitions share a similar structure, but the occasion determines which of the three stages predominates. For rituals associated with death it is separation, and for marriage, incorporation.

This process of social transition is described in spatial or territorial terms. The word 'passage' indicates spatial movement, and deliberate purposeful movement at that. The middle stage in van Gennep's scheme, liminality, uses the threshold of a house as an image to describe territory that belongs neither to the household nor to the outside world. Social movement is analogous to departure from home territory, passage through a 'no man's land', and acceptance in a strange territory. The rite of passage is a similarly hazardous journey. Performing the correct rituals may be intended to invoke supernatural assistance, but also defines a person's social status at any given time.

Van Gennep has been enormously influential, not least in the context of the revision of Christian pastoral rites. It is easy to see why this might be the case. The three stages of rites of passage are clearly discernible in Christian rites. In marriage, a couple first 'get engaged', whereupon they enter a liminal state of 'engagement' when they are neither married nor single. This period ends when the couple get married, and they acquire the social status of married persons. This whole process is marked by a series of familiar ritual actions, and by the deployment of familiar symbolic objects. Similar things can be said of the rites associated with death. However, we should exercise some caution. It is easy to see in theories of ritual such as this something comparable with a medical discovery: if we know how something works, we can correct faults when things go wrong. Van Gennep, as a social scientist, was interested in describing social behaviour, not in making suggestions about how rites 'ought' to work. As a social functionalist, he was interested in how social stability was maintained in the face of the inevitable disruptions of the human life-cycle. He did not draw up a blueprint for a successful rite of passage, which, if followed, would ensure the effectiveness of the rite, in terms of the maintenance of personal or social equilibrium. What we can usefully take from van Gennep's work on this area is that ritual associated with life crises is nearly universal, an important aspect of human social life, and that rites associated with major events in life are often complex and long-drawn-out affairs.

Pastoral rites and the Christian life

Christian pastoral rites may well be an example of a broader category of rites of passage, but they are something of an anomaly within Christian liturgical practice, a fact which needs to be addressed briefly. There has always existed within Christianity a thread of scepticism about the importance of the ordinary life-cycle for the Christian life. The physical is unimportant in comparison with spiritual life in Christ, the social of little significance when contrasted with the Kingdom of God and its precursor, the Church. According to this understanding of Christian discipleship, a person's physical or social status is of minimal importance to his or her relationship to God, through Christ. The nature of Christian worship owes much to this kind of insight. The Eucharist and the daily office point to Christ, and to the centrality of his story for the life of the Christian and the Church. Baptism concerns the conferring of Christian identity, and the priority of that identity over any other that may lay claim to an individual.

The problem with this separation of the business of Christianity from the rest of human life is that it overlooks three important facts. First, members of the Church have ordinary, bodily lives, which they live in a particular social and cultural context. Second, Christianity rejects 'the world and the flesh', but nevertheless ascribes considerable importance to the body, in the doctrines of creation, the incarnation and the resurrection, and in the standards of behaviour demanded of Christians. Lastly, no idea, however world-denying, can be expressed in anything other than human language, and human language is not simply a matter of the clear labelling of discrete objects and notions. Language is descriptive, but also evocative and effective. It indicates connections between things and it can change those connections. In other words language is not just a matter of signs but of symbols (to employ the taxonomy introduced in Chapter 1 by Christopher Irvine). Symbols are verbal or material objects or actions possessed of layers of meaning, acquired by repeated use, both metaphorical and metonymic, in particular cultural contexts, in other words in the telling of stories. Stories gain their power by deploying symbols, and symbols can be seen as the distilled essence of stories. So Christian discourse must employ language, and Christian ritual must employ symbols and actions, that are also put to many other uses. In so doing, of course, the Christian narrative leaves its own mark on these things it thus employs, adding layers of specifically Christian meaning to symbols, as well as to words and concepts.

This has great importance for the development of pastoral rites. These have developed because of the first two of these facts. The very existence of Christian pastoral rites indicates, indeed symbolizes, a positive theological estimation of ordinary, embodied life. This is of enormous importance. The most significant symbolism of any church wedding or funeral is that it takes place within an act of Christian worship and within consecrated space. In addition, such rites form a part of pastoral ministry, and their proper performance cannot be separated from that. For a wedding or funeral to 'work' in symbolic terms, it must be a part of caring and conscientious pastoral ministry. The third fact goes some way to accounting for the character of pastoral rites. They are laden with symbols – objects, actions, and words too – which carry a substantial weight of accrued meaning well beyond mere semantics. Not all of this symbolism relates to the Christian tradition. Weddings and funerals are what Douglas Davies refers to as 'dual, or multi-purpose rites' (Davies 2002: pp. 120ff.) serving different purposes simultaneously, in this case being both Christian liturgy and social rite of passage.

Performance

An important aspect of symbolism 'working' is performance. There is a considerable volume of material on this subject, much of which derives from the collaboration between Richard Schechner, a theatre studies specialist, and Victor Turner, an anthropologist (see Turner and Bruner 1986, *The Anthropology of Experience*; Schechner 1988, 1993). Most relevant for present purposes is Schechner's idea of 'the performance'. For Schechner, performance is a special kind of deliberate action. It includes theatrical performances and religious ritual, though it extends into broader areas of social life; but a theatrical performance is a good model for the wider phenomenon. A performance is framed in time and space: it has a beginning and an end, and clearly demarcated space in which it takes place. Within the time frame and space, distinct roles are allocated and undertaken for the duration of the performance. A performance 'works' where these roles, and the ordering of time and space for the sake of the performance, are sustained. Pastoral rites are like this. A wedding or a funeral is just that – a wedding or a funeral, a set-piece performance, extraordinarily familiar in structure, but also, because of the participants, completely unique. If we can understand pastoral rites as performances, this makes sense of the instinct that it really matters how carefully things are done. The appearance of all the participants, including the minister, is important, as is movement into, out of and around the liturgical space. These things need to be purposeful, but inconspicuous. The minister in a pastoral rite is there to fulfil a role for the benefit of people at a critical point in their lives, not to display deliberately or carelessly their own personality. The realities of a funeral offer little temptation to do any such thing. A wedding is rather different and perhaps herein lies the reason why weddings, but never funerals, have rehearsals.

Weddings

Symbolism in wedding rites may well have its origins outside of the Christian tradition. Processions, flowers, special clothes and feasting are aspects of all wedding rites. Because of the familiarity of the wedding rite well beyond the bounds of worshipping members of the Church, liturgical symbols often acquire meanings in addition to those which the Church might wish to promote. It must be said that there is no one account of marriage from a Christian point of view. In part this is because, unlike birth or death, marriage is not an incontrovertible physical fact which people must attempt to come to terms with. It is a shifting state of life, institution and relationship, given by God or constructed by social processes, through which glimpses of the Kingdom of God, of the relation between Christ and the Church, might sometimes be seen. It is a contract, a covenant, a sacrament, a commonwealth (Witte, 1997). It is the property of the weak, who cannot endure celibacy, or the strong, who can resist promiscuity. It is the business of the Church or the business of the state or the business of families or of the couple alone. This encourages the universal tendency for weddings to acquire additional rites and layer after layer of secondary symbolism. And, on the whole, people find this helpful, emphasizing the importance of their change of status.

Historical development of marriage liturgy

Christian liturgical texts relating to marriage date from the fourth century AD, and there is even earlier evidence of some sort of liturgical involvement in marriage. In Britain, as in the West more generally, the Church had effective legal control of the institution of marriage from the time of Charlemagne to the Hardwicke Act of 1754, which, ironically, also required, for the first time, that all people, excepting only Quakers and Jews, should contract their marriages according to specifically Christian, indeed Church of England rites. The lack of *requirement* to have a church wedding did not prevent the development of a rich body of relevant liturgical material. Stevenson (1982, 1987) offers comprehensive accounts of the development of marriage liturgy, and a concise account can be found in Bradshaw (2006: pp. 180–4). Several observations about the use of symbolism in wedding liturgy are relevant here. The first is the very act of bringing the marriage into church. The earliest pastoral advice for marrying Christians was simply to come to church soon after the wedding to receive a nuptial blessing at the ordinary celebration of the Eucharist. Now a great deal could be said about what blessing is, and how it might work. There is not the room to do this here. Suffice it to say that physical realities are important. A nuptial blessing is not delivered at a distance. The couple must enter the physical space of the church building, in a specifically liturgical setting. They must kneel and have the priest pray over them. This is not to say that the choreography is intrinsic to the efficacy of the blessing, but an important symbolism is at work: the marriage enters physically and by implication spiritually into the worshipping reality of the Church. The same is true of liturgical material called the 'domestic blessings', also dating from the fourth century: prayers and blessings of the future couple's house and bed. Again, ordinary things are offered to and received back from God. Like blessings, wedding vows are performative utterances – not simple statements of fact or intent, but effective actions in speech form (Austin 1962). The wedding vow is a relatively late feature of wedding liturgy, originating in northern Europe early in the twelfth century, prompted by the fact that canon law asserted that it was the mutual consent of the couple that effected the marriage. Two sets of vows developed – the first being declarations of intent to marry, in effect betrothal, and the second being the vows proper, promises to marry right now. Canon law for a long time held that betrothal (i.e. a promise to marry in the future) between persons canonically free to marry each other, followed by cohabitation, constituted a binding marriage. Like the blessing, the wedding vow, a legal statement in words, is still an important symbol. It operates as a metonym – the part standing for the complex whole. The evocative quality of a wedding is, in large part, focused on the vows. They are probably the piece of English prose in longest continuous liturgical use – wedding vows having been in the vernacular long before any other liturgical formulae. The vows stand for the whole wedding, and indeed the whole quality of commitment of a relationship. The words are so familiar that phrases and even single words stand for the whole vow.

Not only does the service as a whole, particularly the vows, have a symbolic resonance, but wedding liturgy has included symbols more conventionally understood as well. These will be discussed in the following consideration of symbolism in the *Common Worship (CW)* service. They include rings, flowers, canopies, the exchange of gold and gifts, the binding of the couple with the priest's stole, special clothing, liturgical movement, and feasting. It should be pointed out at this stage that the inclusion of these things within the wedding service, or even as a part of the continuing wedding celebrations after the liturgy has been concluded, have been at times controversial, and not only in the sweeping liturgical upheavals of the Reformation.

Common Worship

Throughout the rest of this chapter, except where indicated, page references will be to *Common Worship: Pastoral Services*.

The basic structure of the *CW* service makes a sharp distinction between the declarations and the vows. The former is followed in the Introduction by the collect, readings and sermon, before the Marriage proper in the second section. The principle at work is to distinguish what is left of the betrothal from the wedding, marking the earlier historical distinction. There are moves in some quarters to extend the liturgical involvement in marriage, with rites for betrothal removed to the time of engagement or even, perhaps, to the time of setting up home together prior to marriage (see Stevenson 1987 and Thatcher 1999 for arguments that support these respective positions). The very start of the service reflects this sort of tension. The text begins with the minister's Welcome, though it is conventional that this is preceded by the bridal procession. The groom and best man are already in the church at the front, and the bride enters, following the minister, usually escorted by her father or another male (or much less frequently, female) relative. She is then 'given away' immediately after the declarations or before the vows. There has been considerable effort to discourage the idea of 'giving away' in favour of one of escorting. The intention is to emphasize the equality of bride and groom and then husband and wife, and to discourage the notion that the bride is the property either of her father or her husband. Lack of enthusiasm for alternatives among marrying couples should not, in my view, be taken to indicate that they do not believe in equality between the sexes. The point is – and it is an important point when considering symbolism in pastoral rites – that the powerfully symbolic action of a bride being escorted to her future husband by a close relative can be read in more than one way. It would be impossible to generalize, but one level on which this might work is that the giving away is a part of it being done 'properly', of having one's own wedding be an authentic performance of 'the wedding', and doing things properly is a vital part of the reason why people get married in church, when they are not habitual churchgoers. The Church is quick to note the overweening individualism of contemporary society. But there remain strong bonds between most parents and children throughout their lives, and actions which symbolize this, and take account of it at critical moments, however inadequately, should be altered only very carefully. The alternative question and response put to the parents of both bride and bridegroom (p. 133) might be a way forward here, allowing for gradual change.

The dress of the couple is something that clergy doubtless notice, but on which the Church holds no formal view. The long white dress, introduced by Queen Victoria, is still the overwhelmingly popular choice, though not perhaps as universal as it once was. White is taken to indicate the virginity of the bride, though there is good reason to believe that white wedding dresses became popular because they were as suggestive of wealth as of virginity. One could argue that in the contemporary world, where few brides are virgins, this symbolism is spectacularly inappropriate, especially since it concentrates on the bride, and takes no interest in the groom. Again, the continued observance of this custom results from a desire to do things 'properly', of performance. A white (or distinctive) wedding dress indicates more than the sexual history of the bride – it indicates who the bride is. It is for this reason that it is seen as very bad form to wear white to someone else's wedding. The groom's clothes are less distinctive; very often his dress hardly differs from that of the best man and other key male figures, and it is much plainer than the bride's. Interestingly, this is changing, and there is some evidence of a return to pre-Victorian flamboyant male dress.

So the key participants are in place. The guests are seated in approximate order of importance in relation to the bride and groom, and the service starts with extended speech, in sober and serious tone. This is not an exclusive characteristic of a Christian wedding service – civil ceremonies differ not so much in tone as in content. In this speech the Christian possibilities of marriage are described. However rich the symbolism in marriage it has never been allowed to speak entirely for itself. The solemn, legal tone in the reading of the banns persists in the couple's declarations. This section is concluded with a silent prayer and a collect. There then follows a Ministry of the Word, making the rite an act of Christian worship.

The Marriage proper follows. The couple stand before the minister. The focus is now firmly and more intensively on the couple. The rubric says that the bride and bridegroom are to face each other, and the bridegroom is to take the right hand of the bride in his. It is here that the giving away generally happens. It is a somewhat unnatural and awkward manoeuvre – placing the hand of the bride into that of the minister, who puts it into the hand of the groom – and it needs to be done so as not to be too distracting. There are echoes in this action of both informal affectionate hand-holding and, more, of formal, respectful hand-shaking, and of something greater than either – the movement from one social status and set of allegiances to another, at an intimate level. It is not that the priest (or deacon) effects the marriage by his or her actions at this point (or any other). In western Christian thinking it is always the couple who marry each other, the minister witnessing the action on behalf of the Church and the state, and blessing it. But here the minister represents the Church, in the service of people in the course of their lives. It is at this point that a priest may bind the couple's joined hands with his or her stole, or any minister place his or her hand on the joined hands of the couple, either action underlining both the hand-holding and the involvement of the Church. The couple bring their mutual consent and commitment into the presence of God in an act of Christian worship, however tentatively, and God is present in their exchange of vows.

Following the vows is the exchange of rings. Rings have been a symbol in Christian weddings as long as there have been Christian weddings – although there were periods during and after the Reformation when rings were not used in English weddings, following a wider suspicion about symbolism and ritual, due partly to the association of such things with rejected Catholic practice, and partly to a more positive commitment to clarity of meaning in worship. (Any attempt to Christianize the symbolism of marriage must accept that symbols are, by definition, opaque and open to various interpretations.) Still, the exchange of rings has persisted as the only mandatory symbolic act in the marriage rite. The minister prays over the rings, describing them explicitly as a '*symbol* of unending love and faithfulness' (p. 109; italics mine) or '*symbols* to remind them of the covenant made this day' (p. 151; italics mine); the rubric specifies on which finger the ring is to be worn and it is placed there by the other spouse, with a verbal formula which expresses the symbolic value of the ring and then builds on the promises made in the vows. The now common custom of both partners wearing rings is commended as indicating an equality between the spouses, though provision is made for only the bride to have a ring. Not only does the ring symbolize permanence (a ring is a never-ending circle) and faithfulness, but also the mutual sharing of wealth. Stephen Lake (2000: 97) suggests introducing at this point in the service an old rite of the exchange of coins, symbolizing mutual wealth. Like the vows, the *CW* ring exchange formulae are egalitarian; both husband and wife make the same commitment. The general pattern is that the husband makes his promises first, but it is specified that this need not be the case. It is still possible for wives to promise to obey, as well as love and cherish, their husbands.

The wedding is then proclaimed by the minister, who introduces his action and, holding their hands together, pronounces them married. The nuptial blessing follows, which is regarded by Kenneth Stevenson (1983) as the central act of the marriage liturgy. The marriage is generally registered at this point, though it can be done at the end of the service. Prayers follow, and a final dismissal, and then the procession out, this time with the bride and groom together. Where a wedding takes place within a Eucharist, symbolism differs little, but the whole service underlines the location of the wedding within Christian worship, and by implication the location of the marriage within the Christian community.

Other symbolic actions could be introduced into weddings. The North American custom of lighting candles on a three-candle stand is gaining some ground. Here the outer two candles, standing for either the bride and groom as individuals, or their families, are lit, early in the service, by either the couple themselves or relatives. After the vows the couple each light a taper from 'their candle' and together light the central candle. The lighting of a 'wedding candle' can also mark the transition from the wedding to the prayers in the rite, with the couple lighting tapers and together lighting a single candle prominently placed on the altar as the minister calls the congregation to prayer. Candles can also be lit after the Welcome, as a way of remembering close relatives who have died. Of the numerous symbolic actions and words, some speak more powerfully than others to particular people.

Giving active roles to many in a service might help more people engage with it, as well as symbolically marking degrees of intimacy with the couple. Candle ceremonies not only focus moments of prayer but also may indicate the importance of the networks of family and friends which are celebrated and defined in a wedding.

Many couples getting married now have children, and these should be included in the wedding. This will often be as attendants. Here a canopy, held over the couple as they make their vows in both Jewish and some Lutheran weddings, and including the children, might be profitably employed. It is also increasingly the case that children are baptized at the wedding of their parents, which necessitates some care in planning the service, but which can certainly emphasize the Christian symbolism of the wedding rite.

Funerals and pastoral ministry

Funerals, like weddings, are a universal feature of human societies. In normal circumstances human beings do not simply dispose of bodies without a ritual marking of the event. As for weddings, the simple fact of conducting a funeral in the form of an act of Christian worship has enormous symbolic importance. The physical reality of death is brought into a context in which the Paschal mystery of Christ's death and resurrection is declaimed and ritualized.

If weddings raise tricky questions for the Church about the relation of the Church and the surrounding culture, funerals are even more demanding. It is the purpose of a Christian funeral to articulate both the reality of death and bereavement and the Christian hope of resurrection, to remember and celebrate the life of the person who has died (although this aspect has by no means always been seen as important, or even proper), to dispose of their body reverently and to commend their soul to the care and mercy of God, in Christ. This is no easy task, and it makes considerable demands of the minister, as both a pastor and a liturgical celebrant.

The funeral rites assume Christian faith, in some measure, on the part of the departed, and speak explicitly of the hope of the resurrection. As for weddings, there is evidence of Christian liturgy associated with death from early in the life of the Church. The overall movement of such early funerals seems to have some things in common with weddings. The funeral ceremony began at the home of the deceased, with a procession with the body from there to the grave, often by way of the church. As for marriage, the elaborate rites in existence at the time of the Reformation were subject to radical revision by the reformers, in line with their liturgical reform more generally. Following the practice of the Book of Common Prayer (BCP) and the *Alternative Service Book (ASB)*, *Common Worship* offers not just a funeral service, but a staged sequence of rites. There are also rites for use with the dying (pp. 235ff.), before the funeral and after the funeral, including outlines for memorial services. In addition, All Souls' Day services are often used in parishes as a pastoral rite.

Staged rites

This staged sequence of rites, not all of which, of course, are always required, is again suggestive of van Gennep's rites of passage. The Church probably has greater influence over proceedings in funerals than in weddings. Funerals are not legal ceremonies, effecting a legal change of status. A greater proportion of funerals are conducted by ministers of the Church of England than are weddings, and many of the aspects of the contemporary wedding that the Church might be uncomfortable with are not an issue in funerals. But there is another side to the coin. While cohabiting and divorced people planning to marry will, very often, be pleased and relieved to find a sympathetic minister, expectations of the minister at the time of death will be greater, and many of these will simply be assumed. Customs vary according to region, and ministers who move about can encounter completely unfamiliar expectations in terms of when to visit and how long to stay. Moreover, funerals happen with scant notice, and cannot be timed to suit the convenience of anyone, least of all the minister.

As with weddings, indeed even more so, a funeral cannot be done well without a considerable investment of time and effort, not simply into planning the service, but into the pastoral care of the bereaved family, and very often the dying person. Getting the performance of the funeral 'right' is a part of this pastoral concern, not a substitute for it. I will consider the symbolism that is and might be employed when using the material in *Pastoral Services* (pp. 216–401).

Common Worship

The first service is Ministry at the Time of Death (pp. 216–35). This involves a private rite of penitence and reconciliation, with just the dying person and the minister present, after which more people can be included if desired. Here there are prayers, readings, laying on of hands and anointing with consecrated oil, if the minister is a priest, and Holy Communion. This whole rite is unequivocal in both words used and symbolism employed. It points to the possibility of reconciliation with God, and with other people, in Christ. It employs anointing, and points, therefore, towards other liturgical occasions at which people are anointed. It includes either the celebration of the Eucharist, or just the receiving of communion, which includes the rite in the central act of Christian worship, and includes the dying person in the death and resurrection of Christ, which are made present in this central liturgical act.

Prayers are supplied for private use by the bereaved; at the time of death, there is a short service which can be conducted at home before the funeral and prayers that can be said by those unable to attend the funeral. None of these employ symbolism to any notable extent, except in the sense that an extended series of rites, in the liminal period between a death and the conclusion of the funeral, may provide occasions for people to express their grief and loss.

Many funerals conducted according to the rites of the Church of England are held at crematoria or graveyards, without a separate service in church. Most, however, involve a church service and then a committal before the body is buried or cremated. The journey of the body to the funeral is of considerable symbolic importance. Sometimes the body is taken to church from the house. At other times it is brought from the funeral directors'. Sometimes the body is brought to the church in advance of the actual funeral, often the night before. It is received by the minister at the door of the church and escorted, sometimes preceded by someone carrying a candle, preferably the Paschal candle, representing the power of the risen Christ over death, into the body of the church. The coffin may be sprinkled with water, in memory of the deceased's baptism and, when in place, covered by a pall. A cross, a Bible and other 'symbols of the life and faith of the departed' (p. 244) may be placed on or near the coffin. This is the symbolism of a final journey, but a journey accompanied by loved ones into the care of Christ. People may sit with the coffin, in some cases through the night. Forms are given for a funeral vigil.

The funeral itself begins, like the wedding and like other acts of worship, with the gathering of the congregation, which in itself can be understood as symbolizing the corporate nature of our human identity, and specifically that of the Church. Again, as for a wedding, those closest to the deceased sit nearest to the centre of the liturgical action, in this case, the body. R. Anne Horton observes that 'the body is a natural point of focus for symbolic action' (Horton 2000: p. 135) and this is an important point. The death of the body is the occasion for the funeral, but nevertheless the body represents the person, and its ultimate burial or cremation very often brings home the reality of their death. The funeral itself is a service of prayers and readings, commending the departed to the mercy of God and committing the body to burial or cremation. Again, movement in physical space stands for movement in terms of the circumstances of life.

Special provision is made for funerals for children and for those who have died violently. In both these cases the provision is deliberately crafted to articulate the additional shock and grief occasioned by deaths even more disturbing and distressing than usual.

Also of relevance to funeral rites is the common practice of inviting bereaved people to services on All Souls' Day (2 November), or around this season of remembrance. The service may be a Eucharist or a Service of the Word. After the readings and short homily members of the congregation may be invited to the front of the church to light a candle to remember their departed loved one, possibly as the choir sings appropriate words, such as a plainsong *Requiem aeternum*, the Russian Contakion of the Dead (*New English Hymnal* 526), or the Taizé chant, 'Jesus, remember me when you come into your kingdom'. Such liturgical provision symbolizes, as well as practically contributing to, the continued pastoral care of the Church, which should be evident throughout pastoral rites.

Pastoral rites are familiar rituals that help people to accept that they have entered a new period of their lives. Possible meanings of individual symbols are secondary to the occasion as a whole. To ask what symbolism is for in wedding or funeral rites is to ask a non-question. Rites use symbolism in the way that speech uses words. But 'doing it properly' matters in these areas of life. That is not because a well-conducted wedding will make the resulting marriage happier, or a well-conducted funeral will take the sting out of death. This is asking too much. What a pastoral rite can do is to give voice to what is otherwise impossible, or very hard to articulate, in the hope that the action will 'speak louder than words', when the words at one's ordinary disposal are just not enough.

Sources and further reading

The following is not an exhaustive bibliography on liturgical symbols, but lists some major sources and texts which are relevant to that topic.

Alexander, Neil J. (ed.), *Time and Community* (Washington DC: Pastoral Press, 1990).

Alexander, Neil J., *Waiting for the Coming: The Liturgical Meaning of Advent, Christmas and Epiphany* (Washington, DC: Pastoral Press, 1993).

The Alternative Service Book 1980 (Oxford: Mowbray and Oxford University Press, 1980).

Andrewes, Lancelot, 'The Order for Consecrating Plate for the Altar', in P. E. More and F. L. Cross (eds), *Anglicanism* (London: SPCK, 1935), pp. 547–9.

Atchley, E. G., Cuthbert F., *A History of the Use of Incense in Divine Worship* (London: Longmans, 1909).

Auden, W. H., 'In Memory of W. B. Yeats', in *W. H. Auden: Collected Poems*, ed. Edward Mendelson (London: Faber and Faber, 1991), p. 249.

Austin, J. L., *How to Do Things With Words* (Oxford: Clarendon Press, 1962).

Baptism, Eucharist and Ministry, WCC Faith and Order Paper 111 (Geneva: World Council of Churches, 1982).

Bradshaw, Paul (ed.), *A Companion to Common Worship*, vol. 1 (London: SPCK, 2001).

Bradshaw, Paul (ed.), *A Companion to Common Worship*, vol. 2 (London: SPCK, 2006).

Bradshaw, Paul, *Ordination Rites of the Ancient Churches of East and West* (Collegeville, Minn.: Pueblo, 1990).

Buchanan, Colin, *The Renewal of Baptismal Vows* (Nottingham: Grove Books, 1993).

Caldecott, Stratford (ed.), *Beyond the Prosaic: Renewing the Liturgical Movement* (Edinburgh: T&T Clark, 1998).

Carr, Wesley, *Brief Encounters: Pastoral Ministry through Baptisms, Weddings and Funerals* (London: SPCK, 1994).

Cassirer, Ernst, *Language and Myth*, tr. Susanne K. Langer (New York: Dover Books, 1953).

Celebrating Common Prayer (London: Mowbray, 1992).

Chauvet, Louis-Marie, *The Sacraments: The Word of God at the Mercy of the Body* (Collegeville, Minn.: Liturgical Press, 2001).

Chauvet, Louis-Marie, *Symbol and Sacrament* (Collegeville, Minn.: Pueblo, 1995).

Chupungco, Anscar J., *Handbook for Liturgical Studies: Fundamental Liturgy* (Collegeville, Minn.: Liturgical Press, 1998).

Common Worship: Christian Initiation (London: Church House Publishing, 2005).

Common Worship: Daily Prayer (London: Church House Publishing, 2005).

Common Worship: Initiation Services (London: Church House Publishing, 1998).

Common Worship: Ministry to the Sick (London: Church House Publishing, 2000).

Common Worship: Pastoral Services (London: Church House Publishing, 2000).

Common Worship: Times and Seasons (London: Church House Publishing, 2006).

Corbin, Alan, *Foul and Fragrant: Odour and the Social Imagination* (London: Macmillan, 1996).

Coyle, Tom (ed.), *Christian Ministry to the Sick* (London: Cassell, 1986).

Cramer, Peter, *Baptism and Change in the Early Middle Ages c.200–c.1150* (Cambridge: Cambridge University Press, 1993).

Daniélou, Jean, *Primitive Christian Symbols*, tr. Donald Attwater (London: Burns and Oates, 1964).

Davies, Douglas J., *Anthropology and Theology* (Oxford: Berg, 2002).

Davies, J. Douglas, *Cremation Today and Tomorrow*, Joint Liturgical Study 16 (Nottingham: Grove Books, 1990).

Day, Juliette, *Baptism in Early Byzantine Palestine 325–451*, Joint Liturgical Study 43 (Cambridge: Grove Books, 1999).

Dearmer, Percy, *The Parson's Handbook*, 12th edn (London: Oxford University Press, 1932).

Dendy, D. R., *The Use of Lights in Christian Worship* (London: SPCK, 1959).

Dillistone, F. W., *Christianity and Symbolism* (London: SCM Press, 1985).

Dillistone, F. W., *The Power of Symbols* (London: SCM Press, 1986).

Douglas, Mary, *Natural Symbols* (Harmondsworth: Penguin Books, 1978).

Dudley, Martin, and Rowell, Geoffrey (eds), *The Oil of Gladness: Anointing in the Christian Tradition* (London: SPCK, 1993).

Dupré, Louis, *Symbols of the Sacred* (Grand Rapids, Mich.: Eeerdmans, 2000).

Eliade, Mircea, *Birth and Rebirth* (London: Harvill Press, 1961).

Eliade, Mircea, *The Sacred and the Profane: The Nature of Religion*, tr. Willard R. Trask (San Diego: Harcourt Brace Jovanovich, 1959).

Fisch, Thomas (ed.), *Liturgy and Tradition: Theological Reflections of Alexander Schmemann* (Crestwood, NY: St Vladimir's Seminary Press, 1990).

Fortescue, Adrian, and O'Connell, J., *The Ceremonies of the Roman Rite Described*, 8th edn (London: Burns, Oates and Washbourne, 1948).

General Synod of the Church of England, *Report of Proceedings*, vol. 13 (London: Church Information Office, 1982).

Gordon-Taylor, Benjamin, and Jones, Simon, *Celebrating the Eucharist*, Alcuin Liturgy Guide 3 (London: SPCK, 2005).

Grimes, Ronald L., *Deeply into the Bone: Reinventing Rites of Passage* (Berkeley: University of California Press, 2000).

Guardini, Romano, *The Spirit of the Liturgy* (London: Sheed and Ward, 1930).

Harford, G., Stevenson, M., and Tyron, G. M. (eds), *The Prayer Book Dictionary* (London: Pitman, 1912).

Heaney, Seamus, 'Crossings xxxii', in *Seeing Things* (London: Faber and Faber, 1991), p. 90.

Holton, David (ed.), *Growing in Newness of Life: Christian Initiation in Anglicanism Today* (Toronto: Anglican Book Centre, 1993).

Horton, R. Anne, *Using Common Worship: Funerals* (London: Church House Publishing, 2000).

Irvine, Christopher, *The Art of God: The Making of Christians and the Meaning of Worship* (London: SPCK, 2005).

Irvine, Christopher (ed.), *Celebrating the Easter Mystery: Worship Resources from Easter to Pentecost* (London: Mowbray, 1996).

Jeanes, Gordon P., *The Day Has Come: Easter and Baptism in Zeno of Verona* (Collegeville, Minn.: Liturgical Press, 1995).

Johnson, Maxwell E., *The Rites of Christian Initiation: Their Evolution and Interpretation* (Collegeville, Minn.: Pueblo, 1999).

Johnson, Maxwell E., and Phillips, L. Edward (eds), *Studia Liturgica Diversa: Essays in Honor of Paul F. Bradshaw* (Portland, Ore.: Pastoral Press, 2004).

Jung, Carl G., *Man and his Symbols* (London: Aldus Books, 1979).

Kavanagh, Aidan, *The Shape of Baptism: The Rite of Christian Initiation* (New York: Pueblo, 1978).

Kavanagh, Aidan, 'Textuality and Deritualization: The Case of Western Liturgical Usage', *Studia Liturgica* 23.1 (1993), pp. 70–7.

Lake, Stephen, *Using Common Worship: Marriage* (London: Church House Publishing, 2000).

Lathrop, Gordon W., *Holy Ground: A Liturgical Cosmology* (Minneapolis: Fortress, 2003).

Leach, John, *How to Use Symbol and Action in Worship* (Cambridge: Grove Books, 2005).

Ligier, Louis, 'The Biblical Symbolism of Baptism in the Fathers and in the Liturgy', *Concilium* 22 (1967), pp. 16–30.

Lockett, William, *The Modern Architectural Setting of the Liturgy* (London: SPCK, 1964).

Lukken, Gerrard, *Rituals in Abundance: Critical Reflections on the Place, Form and Identity of Christian Ritual in our Culture* (Leuven: Peeters, 2005).

Macgregor, A. J., *Fire and Light in the Western Triduum: Their Use at Tenebrae and at the Paschal Vigil* (Collegeville, Minn.: Liturgical Press, 1992).

Madden, Lawrence J., *The Awakening Church: 25 Years of Liturgical Renewal* (Collegeville, Minn.: Liturgical Press, 1992).

McGuckin, John Anthony, *At the Lighting of the Lamps: Hymns of the Ancient Church* (Oxford: SLG Press, 1995).

McIntyre, John, *Theology After the Storm: Reflections on the Upheavals in Modern Theology and Culture* (Grand Rapids, Mich.: Eerdmans, 1997).

Merton, Thomas, *Disputed Questions* (London: Hollis and Carter, 1960).

Mitchell, Leonel L., *Worship: Initiation and the Churches* (Portland, Ore.: Pastoral Press, 1991).

New Patterns for Worship (London: Church House Publishing, 2002).

On the Way: Towards an Integrated Approach to Christian Initiation (London: Church House Publishing, 1995).

Perham, Michael, *A Handbook of Pastoral Liturgy* (London: SPCK, 2000).

Pickstock, Catherine, *After Writing: On the Liturgical Consummation of Philosophy* (Oxford: Blackwell, 1998).

Power, David N., *Unsearchable Riches: The Symbolic Nature of Liturgy* (Collegeville, Minn.: Pueblo, 1984).

The Promise of His Glory (London: Church House Publishing and Mowbray, 1991).

Rappaport, Roy A., *Ritual and Religion in the Making of Humanity* (Cambridge: Cambridge University Press, 1999).

Ricœur, Paul, *The Symbolism of Evil* (Boston: Beacon Press, 1967).

Ritual Notes (London: W. Knott and Son, 1947, 1956).

Roll, Susan K., *Towards the Origins of Christmas* (Kampen: Kok Pharos, 1995).

Rotelle, John E., 'The Commemoration of Baptism in the Life of the Christian', *Ephemerides Liturgicae* 86 (1972), pp. 475–85.

Rowell, Geoffrey, *The Liturgy of Christian Burial* (London: SPCK, 1977).

Rutherford, Richard, with Barr, Tony, *The Death of a Christian: The Order of Christian Funerals* (Collegeville, Minn.: Pueblo, 1990).

Schechner, Richard, *The Future of Ritual: Writing on Culture* (New York: Routledge, 1993).

Schechner, Richard, *Performance Theory* (New York: Routledge, 1988).

Schmemann, Alexander, *The Eucharist*, tr. Paul Kachur (Crestwood, NY: St Vladimir's Seminary Press, 1987).

Seasoltz, R. Kevin, *A Sense of the Sacred: Theological Foundations of Christian Architecture and Art* (New York: Continuum, 2005).

Sperber, Dan, *Rethinking Symbolism* (Cambridge: Cambridge University Press, 1975).

Spinks, Bryan D., *Early and Medieval Rituals and Theologies of Baptism: From the New Testament to the Council of Trent* (Aldershot: Ashgate, 2006).

Spinks, Bryan D., *Reformation and Modern Rituals and Theologies of Baptism: From Luther to Contemporary Practices* (Aldershot: Ashgate, 2006).

Staley, V. (ed.), *Hierurgia Anglicana*, vol. 2 (London: Alexander Morong, 1902–3).

Stauffer, S. Anita, *On Baptismal Fonts: Ancient and Modern* (Nottingham: Grove Books, 1994).

Stevenson, Kenneth (ed.), *Liturgy Reshaped* (London: SPCK, 1982).

Stevenson, Kenneth, *Nuptial Blessing: A Study of Christian Marriage Rites* (Oxford: Oxford University Press, 1983).

Stevenson, Kenneth W., *To Join Together: The Rite of Marriage* (New York: Pueblo, 1987).

Talley, Thomas J., *The Origins of the Liturgical Year* (New York: Pueblo, 1986).

Thatcher, Adrian, *Marriage After Modernity: Christian Marriage in Postmodern Times* (Sheffield: Sheffield University Press, 1999).

Tillich, Paul, *Theology of Culture* (Oxford: Oxford University Press, 1959).

Torevell, David, *Losing the Sacred* (Edinburgh: T&T Clark, 2000).

Turner, Victor, *The Anthropology of Performance* (New York: PAJ Publications, 1982).

Turner, Victor, *The Forest of Symbols: Aspects of Ndembu Ritual* (London: Cornell University Press, 1967).

Turner, Victor, *From Ritual to Theater: The Human Seriousness of Play* (New York: PAJ Publications, 1982).

Turner, Victor, and Bruner, Edward M., *The Anthropology of Experience* (Chicago: University of Illinois Press, 1986).

van Gennep, Arnold, *The Rites of Passage*, tr. Monika B. Vizedom and Gabrielle L. Caffee (Chicago: University of Chicago Press, 1960; 1st publ. 1908).

Williams, Rowan, *Lost Icons: Reflections on Cultural Bereavement* (Edinburgh: T&T Clark, 2000).

Witte, John, Jr., *From Sacrament to Contract: Marriage and Law in the Western Tradition* (Louisville, Ky: Westminster John Knox Press, 1997).

Woolfenden, G. W., *Daily Liturgical Prayer: Origins and Theology* (Aldershot: Ashgate, 2004).

Index

Index